SAINT JOSÉ

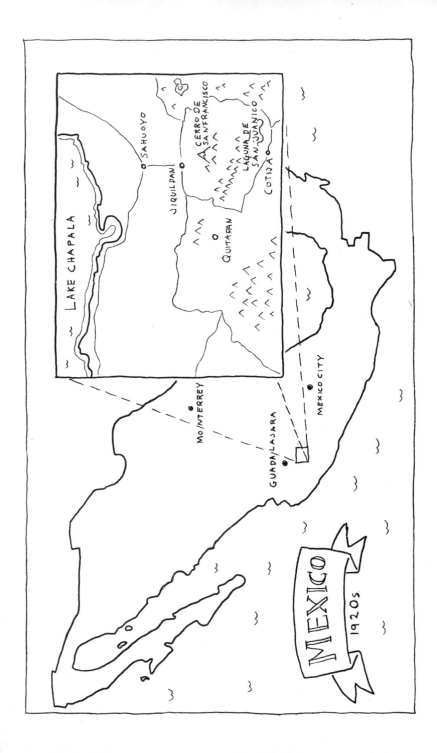

SAINT JOSÉ

Boy Cristero Martyr

Written by

Kevin McKenzie, L.C.

Illustrated by John Herreid

IGNATIUS PRESS   SAN FRANCISCO

Cover art and design by Christopher J. Pelicano

© 2019 by Ignatius Press, San Francisco
ISBN 978-1-62164-242-8
Library of Congress Control Number 2018958976
Printed in the United States of America ∞

To José,
in gratitude

CONTENTS

I

TROUBLE AHEAD

I DARE YOU."

"Oh yeah? Well, I double dare you."

"OK," said José, the taller of the two boys, running a hand through his mop of black hair.

"Last one up for air wins," said his friend Trino.

"One, two, three!" they shouted together.

Both boys took a deep breath, held their noses, and plunged into the slow-moving stream.

It was late July, 1926, in the small town of Sahuayo in central Mexico.

Beneath the surface, the two thirteen-year-olds had opened their eyes. José blew some bubbles, which floated to the surface. Then Trino held his hands up to his head and made a funny face. Next, José gave Trino a push, and soon the two were wrestling underwater.

Bursting to the surface, José was the first to come up for air.

His friend popped up only a second later, gasping for breath.

"No fair, Trino," said José. "We didn't say you could wrestle."

"We didn't say you couldn't," Trino replied with a grin.

"I'm gonna get you!" shouted José as he dove for his friend

Clang, clang, clang went the church bells.

Both boys froze in place.

"Oh no!" groaned José, eyes wide. "We're late for Mass."

~

"You two look like you just finished a marathon," said the priest as he scooped a heaping spoonful of incense onto the glowing charcoal. "Are you ready?"

"*Sí, Padre,*" said José, sweat pouring down his forehead. "This thing is so heavy." He shut the incense-laden censer with a clang. Its thick bronze rings dangled from the boy's fingers, and its weight made his hand droop slowly downward. Smoke poured from its holes, wrapping the two boys and the priest in a heavy cloak.

"Ready . . . when . . . you are, . . . Padre Ignacio," said Trino, who was still catching his breath. He clasped a large processional cross to his chest.

The priest chuckled. "*Bueno*," he said, straightening his vestments. "José, keep that thing open so the smoke can come out, and don't let it touch the ground. Trino, make sure you don't bang Jesus' head on the doorway."

Together, they bowed to the cross and stepped from the sacristy into the church. José walked in front with the incense, Trino followed with the cross, and Padre Ignacio took his place at the rear.

José kept his eyes glued to the smoking censer as it swung back and forth, letting out bursts of thick, perfumed smoke.

From behind he heard a whisper. "Am I supposed to genuflect with this thing?"

"You just bow," replied José, turning his head.

Distracted, he didn't notice the censer drooping. As they neared the altar, its metal base skimmed the surface of the clay tiles, releasing a high-pitched ring.

"Watch out for the step," said Padre Ignacio from behind.

José pulled up on the chain, but he was too late. The censer crashed into the granite step at the foot of the sanctuary.

José watched with dismay as burning charcoal spilled from the open censer and scattered across the floor. Most of it landed harmlessly on the tiles, but one piece bounced its way to the rug beneath the altar. From where it came to rest, smoke billowed up.

"Fire!" cried a voice in the front pew.

~

"José, I thought you were gonna burn the whole church down," said Trino, back in the sacristy, slipping the large cross into its holder.

The sound of chatter came from the back of the church where a small crowd of women and children had gathered after Mass.

"Thank God for holy water," said Padre Ignacio, as he placed his large, white vestment on a hanger.

Laughter filled the sacristy.

José turned to Trino and gave him a jab in the side. "Remember, you were gonna ask," he whispered, raising his eyebrows.

"*You* ask, José—it was your idea," snapped Trino. "Besides, he's *your* uncle."

"*De acuerdo*," said José, sticking a hand in his pocket. "Padre Ignacio, have you ever been up in the bell tower?"

"Of course, José," the priest replied. "What makes you ask?"

"Well, . . . um . . . you . . . see, . . . uh . . . me and Trino—we've been wondering how far you can see from the top."

Padre Ignacio chuckled. "Why on a clear day, you can see all the way to the cathedral in Guadalajara. That's over sixty miles away as the crow flies." A wry smile crossed the priest's face. "Would you like to climb up?"

"Sí, Padre, sí!" the boys blurted out.

"Well then," said the priest, "follow me!"

Turning down a corridor, Padre Ignacio brought them to a gnarled wooden door fastened with an ancient padlock. "Knowing you two," he said, fiddling with the keys, "there's more to this than just the view." He pulled the door open, revealing a spiral staircase.

José drew his hand from his pocket. Trino glanced at him before he admitted sheepishly, "Padre, there is a bet."

José rolled his eyes.

"A bet?" asked Padre Ignacio, arching his eyebrows. "What's at stake?"

"José says he can throw a rock from the top of the tower all the way to his house," Trino replied. "I say he can't. Whoever wins gets to light the candles next time."

Padre Ignacio smiled. "How about we make a deal," he said. "I'll take you to the top of the tower if," he raised his index finger and looked at them sharply, "if you leave your rocks at the bottom."

José cocked his head to the side glumly. "Then who gets to light the candles?"

~

"Look at the lake," said Trino, gazing out from the top of the tower. "It's all sparkling. I've never seen it from this high. Seems like it goes on forever."

"Papá says Lake Chapala is the biggest lake in all of México," said José, holding a hand over his eyes to block the sun. "He says that it used to be even bigger. Sahuayo was a lake town."

"I love Sahuayo just as it is," said Padre Ignacio with a sigh. "Red-roofed houses, lots of trees—small but not too small—it's perfect." His eyes fell lovingly on the town square just below them, with its rows of cedar trees and the large iron gazebo in the center. "Our three churches, Santiago, Sagrado Corazón, and the Santuario," he gazed across town to the other steeple, "make Sahuayo something special. There aren't many three-church towns around."

The figures gazed in silence. Swallows dipped and soared through the warm summer air. Higher still, fluffy clouds drifted across the sky.

"Padre Ignacio, is it true what they say?" asked José.

"About what?" asked the priest.

"That President Calles wants to close the churches?"

"I wish it weren't true," Padre Ignacio said with a sigh. "Calles' new law will make all churches government property—"

"But that's not fair," José broke in.

"—and I won't be allowed to wear my cassock any more. My homilies will need to be approved by the government. Priests can either become employees of the state or leave the country."

"When's all that supposed to happen?" asked Trino.

"Next Sunday, August first."

"Why can't they just leave the Church alone?" fumed José. "Isn't there anything we can do, Padre?"

"Not really—short of all-out war. But the bishops have their own plan. If President Calles goes through with his law on Sunday, they've asked all of us priests to suspend public worship until further notice. They will turn the whole country against Calles."

The Calles Law of 1926

No foreigners can be priests.

Worship outside churches is prohibited.

Religious education is prohibited.

No priests or religious may direct schools.

Taking religious vows is prohibited.

All religious communities are to be dissolved, and community life is prohibited.

Dressing like a priest or religious is prohibited.

Any priest who says that the articles of the Constitution do not oblige under conscience shall be jailed.

Priests are prohibited from criticizing laws in public.

Freedom of the religious press is suppressed.

All churches become property of the state.

The government decides which churches remain open.

All other properties, such as houses of bishops or priests, colleges, seminaries, and convents become property of the state.

No religious association can own or use goods.

No church may be built without authorization of the Secretary of State.

All priests must register with the state government to obtain authorization.

State authorities will decide the maximum number of priests that can minister within their territory.

2

SHOTS IN THE TOWN SQUARE

D ID YOU SEE THE SIGN?" blurted Trino, sombrero
in hand, as he raced around the corner onto Tepeyac Street.

José was sitting in the shade in front of his house.
"What sign?" he asked, looking up at Trino.

The boy leaned heavily against the wall of the house,
catching his breath. "The sign in church over the tabernacle. It says, 'He's not here.'"

José jumped to his feet. "The Eucharist is gone?"

Trino nodded slowly and shrugged his shoulders.

Suddenly, a loud boom split the stillness.

"What was that?" cried Trino, his eyes wide with fear.

"I don't know," growled José. "That was too loud for a firecracker."

A minute later, another loud explosion shattered the dry air.

"Sounds like a gun to me," said Trino, "a *big* gun."

"Yes," added José, "and it's coming from over in the square. Let's go see."

"We'd better stay low," Trino cautioned.

"OK," answered José, "follow me."

As the two boys approached the square, an itch started to grow in Trino's throat. "José," he said, "maybe we shouldn't do this—maybe we should just go home."

"I still think we should go and see," José replied. "Otherwise, we'll never forgive ourselves for being chicken. Come on, follow me. We'll crawl like soldiers."

"If you say so," said Trino, dropping to his knees.

The two slowly made their way down the last street toward the square. Nothing moved on either side.

As they approached the end of the street, the square came into view. In the center rose the tall iron gazebo. To the south, directly across from where they crouched, stood the two-storied Hotel Refugio. To its left sat the Church of Santiago, with its huge bell tower looming over the deserted square.

"*Qué raro*," José whispered. "There's no one out. Feels like Good Friday."

"I wish it were Good Friday," said Trino.

Another bang, this one louder than the last, broke the silence. It came from the direction of the big black gazebo.

"Look," said José. "It's Picazo—moustache man. And he's got help."

José pointed to a figure crouching behind the gazebo. A large black handlebar moustache was plastered across his face. Behind him squatted others, weapons in hand.

"You mean—" Trino was cut short by the crack of another gun from the direction of the church.

"What was that?" asked José, turning around sharply.

"Look, on top of the church," pointed Trino. "Somebody's shooting from the bell tower. He's got a rifle."

"Picazo and his men are trying to take over the church!" exclaimed José. "*Diablos!*"

"I thought he was Catholic!" said Trino, shaking his head.

"At least he's not your godfather," said José bleakly.

Trino slowly turned in surprise. "You mean you're his—"

A loud burst of gunfire jerked his head back.

"It's a shootout," sputtered José.

The firing from both sides grew in volume. Too much was coming from the church for one man. The men stationed behind the gazebo kept firing sporadically.

As the shooting continued, José let out a gasp. Someone had opened the large front door of the church and slipped out to the left.

"It's Padre Ignacio," cried José. "What's he doing?"

"He must be trying to escape," said Trino.

The priest dashed left, his black cassock flapping behind.

"How can he make it?" shouted José. The hail of bullets continued. They ricocheted off the ground and the wall of the church. Suddenly the black cassock stopped and came crashing to the ground.

"No!" cried Trino. "No, it can't be. No!" Tears sprang from his eyes.

"Quiet," barked José, squirming in the dust and grabbing Trino by the shoulder. "Don't get *us* killed too."

"But Padre Ignacio—he's shot! Can't we do something?"

"Here," said José, "let's go around the block. Maybe we can reach him from behind."

Trembling now, Trino nodded.

The two retraced their tracks, backing away from the plaza. Once out of sight of the gazebo, they stood up and ran.

José's heart pounded against his ribs like a sledgehammer. Thoughts raced through his head. *No. No. No! It can't be. Not Padre Ignacio. What had he done? That creep, Picazo, who does he think he is? Mamá will be terrified. Why doesn't anyone do something? Why doesn't somebody stop them?*

The noonday sun cast no shadows on the silent

streets. Quickly they made their way east and then
south in a large loop around the square. At Insurgentes
Avenue, they headed toward the square. Near the end
of the street, the bell tower of the Church of Santiago
reared up on their left.

Slackening their speed as the square drew near, they
hunched down low.

"Where's Padre?" whispered José.

A soft whistle came from the trees beside the church.
The boys turned to look. At the base of a large oak sat
a bundle of black.

"It's Padre Ignacio!" José said, stifling a shout.

With a flutter of his arms, the priest beckoned the
boys over.

They scanned the street for a moment. The gazebo
and Picazo's gunmen were out of sight. They sprinted
to the row of trees.

"You two have a nose for trouble," the priest joked,
as the boys pulled up, breathless.

"*Como está?*" asked José, not noticing the humor.

The priest moved his right leg just enough to reveal
a reddish circle in the dust. "They got me in the calf.
Nothing a couple of stitches can't fix—I hope. I can
still walk a little."

He planted one hand on the tree. "We've got to get
away from the square. Here, help me up."

Each boy grabbed an arm. Soon they had walked the
wounded priest to the end of the street.

"Enough, enough," he said wearily. "I'm out of

danger now." The two boys lowered him to the ground against the wall of a building.

"Was that you back there, Padre Ignacio?" asked Trino, glancing up at the bell tower.

"What, you mean with the rifle?" he answered as his lips grew into a large smile. "No, that's Señor Guízar. He's got a scope too. Not a bad setup. There are five men, all told. I wanted to stay, but they wouldn't have it—said a bottle of tequila would last longer than I would if *los federales* ever got their hands on me."

José spoke up. "Padre, we've got to get you out of here. Want me to bring my horse?"

The priest scratched his head. "I don't know; I wouldn't feel safe that high up."

"How about a wheelbarrow?" asked Trino. "There's one at José's house."

"That sounds better."

José stared at his uncle for a moment. "If you say so," he said, "but you're in for one rough ride. Give us some time, and we'll be right back."

"Fine," said Padre Ignacio, "but be careful. Baptizing you was one thing; I'm not about to say your funeral."

José and Trino took off. They raced down Juárez Avenue until they hit Tepeyac Street.

As they neared the house, José noticed that Trino was falling behind. He slowed so that his friend could catch up. "Should we . . . sneak in the back?" asked Trino.

"No—waste of time," answered José.

"What if your parents stop us?"

"Papá will understand."

The boys ran up to a whitewashed adobe house. From the outside, nothing seemed to be stirring. José banged a fist on the large red door.

"You take one more step, and it'll be your last," announced a gruff voice from inside.

A long rifle barrel protruded from the window on their left.

"Papá, it's me, José."

Don Macario Sánchez poked his head through the window. His short white beard sparkled in the sunlight. "*Madre Santa*, where have you been?" he demanded.

Before José could answer, the front door swung open to reveal José's older brother Miguel. "Mamá has been scared out of her wits over you, José."

"Padre Ignacio's been shot, and he needs help," José said loudly as he and Trino entered the foyer.

"Padre Ignacio? Shot?" cried Don Macario, stepping toward José, still clutching his rifle. "How?" By this time, José's other siblings had started to gather behind their father.

"Padre Ignacio came running out of the church right in the middle of a gunfight," José explained. "They got him in the leg. He sent us to get a wheelbarrow, so we can rescue him. We must hurry."

José ran past his still-astonished father to the courtyard, with Trino and Miguel at his heels. "Where's the wheelbarrow?" he cried. "Miguel, who moved the wheelbarrow?"

Frantically, both boys started running back and forth. Then José slapped a hand to his forehead. "Wait a minute. I know where it is." He hurried over to the chicken coop and pulled open the latch. Birds and feathers went flying in all directions. "Just my luck—they've already turned it into a nest," he exclaimed, grabbing a handful of straw.

Trino helped him scoop out the debris. Then the two began carrying the wheelbarrow through the house.

"Joselito," said a voice, and out of the corner of his eye, José spied a long blue dress.

"Mamá," he said, setting down his end of the wheelbarrow. The boy turned to face his mother and gazed up into her dark brown eyes. Teardrops glistened on Doña Mariquita's face. "Mamá, Padre Ignacio needs our help."

She nodded in agreement. "You be careful, José."

He wrapped his arms around her.

When José and Trino exited the house with the wheelbarrow, Miguel and another older brother, Guillermo, were right behind them. "We're coming with you," said Miguel.

"Good," replied José, smiling.

"Wait a minute, I'm coming too," said Don Macario as he stepped through the doorway, rifle in hand. "No one's going to take another shot at my little brother."

Later that night, the Sánchez del Río family huddled around the priest lying on the couch in their living room.

"Looks like I won't be visiting any sick people for the time being," said Padre Ignacio, giving his bandaged leg a pat.

"As soon as it's safe, we'll take you to Doctor Santos," said Doña Mariquita, who held little Celia, the youngest of her seven children, in her lap. "Until then, you can rest here."

"I can rest, but what about all these bright young minds I see?" asked Padre Ignacio, surveying the children. "After taking over the church, the first thing Picazo did was shut down the school."

"God have mercy on his soul," said Doña Mariquita. "And to think that he used to be our friend, that he is José's godfather."

"Godfather or not, he'll have a lot of reckoning to do when he comes before God," said Don Macario, fingering his snowy-white beard.

"I just hope Trino's safe," broke in José, who sat on the floor at the foot of the couch.

"Where did he end up?" asked Padre Ignacio. "As soon as you had me safe in the wheelbarrow, he took off. I hope he doesn't fall into the hands of the federals. They already killed Señor Ramírez—without a trial."

"Trino told me he was going to check on his family."

Padre Ignacio nodded. Staring up at the ceiling, he let out a sigh, and said, "I wonder what they've done to the church."

"Couldn't anyone defend it?" asked José.

"Señor Degollado did his best. I hear that Amado died right in front of the main door. Even Lola held off Picazo and his gang for a little while. But when the army came, there was nothing to do. They set up their cannons on the hill, and from then on it was either give up or be blown up."

"I knew it was only a matter of time," said Don Macario, "until Picazo would come out of hiding and seek revenge. He's the kind that can't wait."

"He's also the kind that can't tell a jackrabbit from a rattlesnake," said Padre Ignacio. "He and his goons shot little Manuel, Señor Barragán's son, in the first few minutes of the fight. The boy was just trying to make it to safety."

"If these are the people who are supposed to be running Sahuayo," said Don Macario, "then the safest thing we can do is get out of town."

Silence fell. The rays of the setting sun played on the living room wall, and in the courtyard a rooster crowed.

"But why, Padre Ignacio," asked José, "why do they want to take away our churches?"

Padre Ignacio straightened up. He patted the white gauze bandage wrapped around his leg. "Why did they persecute our Lord?" he asked. "I think that's the important question."

"Well," said José, "because he wanted to change things—change things for the better." He looked hopefully at Padre Ignacio.

"Good," the priest replied. "Jesus wanted to start a fire here on earth, a fire that would wake people up. He wanted to deliver them from their slavery to sin and to bring them to heaven. But they didn't understand. His teachings made them feel uncomfortable. Many thought he was crazy." Padre Ignacio paused and then slowly swept his gaze around the room. "If they wanted to kill him, should we—his followers—expect better treatment?

"Ever since México achieved independence," he continued, "there have been struggles between the Church and the government. Fourteen years ago, I and ten other priests were kidnapped and held for ransom, but that was only a regional affair. Now, with President Calles' new law, the government is taking control of the Church throughout the whole country. Calles has named his own 'Mexican Pope'. He's seizing all the churches. He's gone too far.

"Our bishops only had one option left. Instead of allowing the Church to become just another arm of the state, they have decided to suspend all worship. There will be no Mass until the government gives the Church back her freedom."

Padre Ignacio turned to look at José. The boy was staring dreamily at the rifle in the corner. Then he shook his head a moment and said, "But—but Padre, isn't there anything we can do?"

"Yes, there is," said Miguel, clenching his fists. "We can fight back. I think we could beat them."

"I have my suspicions," said Don Macario, "that we won't have long to wait before somebody starts fighting the government. Señor Guízar is now officially an outlaw, as is everyone who helped defend the church today. He'll have to go into hiding or fight. And there are others, though it will take more than just a few to stand up to President Calles and his cronies."

"Who knows what Catholics could do if they decided to resist?" said Padre Ignacio. "I think we don't know how strong we really are."

"I hope that there's no need to find out," said Doña Mariquita with a sigh. "Just give us back our churches, and we'll be happy."

3

THE CRISTEROS

"Mamá, papá, did you hear?" gasped the lanky figure dashing into the room.

Several weeks had passed since the firefight in the town square.

"What? What is it, Miguel?" asked Don Macario, rising from his chair.

Doña Mariquita's eyes darted from Miguel to her husband to José.

"It's—it's Señor Guízar," Miguel said, struggling for

breath. "He's not in hiding. He's fighting back. He's joined up with Señor Ramírez."

"You mean Ignacio Ramírez?" asked Don Macario. "I know Picazo killed his brother, but I never thought Ramírez was the type to take up arms."

"It's not just those two. Señor Ramírez has about three hundred men with him," said Miguel. "What's more, they have a name. They're called the *Cristeros* because their cry is '*Viva Cristo Rey!*'"

"Long live Christ the King! I like it," said Don Macario. "It's about time somebody fought back." He sat down and faced Miguel, now sitting on the floor with his back to the wall. "How did you find out about Señor Guízar?"

Miguel wiped his sweaty brow with his forearm. "I was over at Adán and Guillermo's house," he said. "They're packing right now so they can leave first thing tomorrow morning. They've been accepted into the new army." There was an uncomfortable silence. Miguel stared at his father and added, "I too must join the Cristeros."

"Me too," said Macario. "I'm the oldest son; it's my duty to defend us."

"No!" The shout came from José, who had jumped to his feet.

Doña Mariquita glanced at Don Macario and rose from her chair. "I'll take care of this one," she said. She walked over to José and placed her hands on his shoulders. "Come, my son, let's go upstairs."

José looked at his mother's face and then at his father's, and he knew that there was no point in arguing. Hanging his head, he followed his mother to her room.

"Are you really going to let Miguel and Macario join the Cristeros?" he asked when they were alone.

"I don't know," replied his mother, kissing him on the forehead, "but they are both old enough to fight."

"But they could get killed!" said José, his voice cracking.

His mother's eyes began to glisten. She wrapped her arms around her youngest son and held him tight. "I know," she said softly, "but they must do what they think is right, trusting that their lives are in God's hands. And so must we all."

～

The night slowly slipped away before the dawn as Macario and Miguel, dressed in rusty-brown ponchos, scurried down the lane. In front of the red door to their home, stood their father with his shoulders back and a look of pride mixed with fear on his face. Their mother clutched his side. Her eyes tried to follow her sons, but tears melded everything into one big blur.

José peeked out a window. His fists were clenched into tight balls as he held back his tears.

Macario and Miguel jumped into a donkey cart drawn up against a house further down the road. They covered themselves with a blanket, and the cart rolled off. Before long the cart passed through the city gates. After they were out of sight of anyone who could be stirring at that hour, the two young men slipped from the cart and headed toward the hills south of town.

4

A BIG DECISION

IN THE COURTYARD of the Sánchez del Río house, José was kneeling on the ground. Scratching his short, black hair with his left hand, he leaned forward and placed the knuckle of his right hand on the ground, with the tip of his thumb tucked tightly behind a large red marble. Quickly releasing his thumb, he sent the shiny sphere careening through the cluster of marbles. It struck two smaller marbles, which in turn bounced out of the circle drawn in the dust. José herded them into his pile.

"Not bad," said Trino. "But not good enough. My smasher has been known to cause serious damage. Look."

Trino took aim and let his smasher fly. It bounced off the top of one of the little marbles and then landed outside the circle.

"Nice try," said José, holding his stomach and laughing.

Trino glared back at him.

"Hey, look on the bright side," said José. "At least your smasher didn't get stuck in the middle."

Trino muttered gloomily.

José straightened up. "Let's try this again," he said, launching his smasher once again. This started a chain reaction, causing most of the smaller marbles to roll out of the circle. "Did you see that?" José squealed with delight. He picked up his spoils—nine marbles in all.

Trino lowered his head in dismay and coughed. "Have you heard the news?" he asked.

José froze halfway through his victory celebration and stared at his friend. "No, what news?"

"The Cristeros are accepting boys our age into their army."

A stillness descended upon the courtyard. Even the chickens, as if sensing something was awry, ceased their usual clucking.

"Wait a minute, Trino," said José. "We're only four-teen. When my brothers joined the Cristeros last year they were older than that. Are you sure you heard right?"

"I know I heard right—it was a boy from Jiquilpan who told me. He said the Cristeros need all the help they can get."

They both went silent. On the other side of the courtyard, the clucking started again.

"What do you think?" asked José. "Think they'd accept *us*?"

Trino turned to look at the chickens. "Your parents would let you go, wouldn't they?" he asked.

"I don't know."

What would Mamá and Papá say? José asked himself. *And do I really want to go? I'd miss my family . . . and army life would be hard and . . . I can think up a million reasons not to go.*

"How could we get there?" asked José.

Trino shrugged. "We'd have to write a letter to Gen-eral Ramírez. Then, if he accepted us—"

"*If,*" said José, "that's the question. Would they ac-cept us? I don't know . . ."

Suddenly José wasn't aware of his friend. In his imag-ination he saw his five-year-old self. It was the Mexican Revolution, and Don Macario was moving his family to the city for safety. The wooden cart rattled along be-side the railroad tracks. Doña Mariquita gasped. Peer-ing out, José saw things hanging from the telegraph poles—they were bodies, lots of bodies, as far as he could see. A blanket was thrown over his head, and he saw no more.

Shaking his head free of this horrible memory, José looked around. He would need to give this matter more thought, he realized, and to pray about it too, but not now.

"How about a snack?" he asked Trino. "I think there are some sweets in the kitchen."

~

José leaned all his weight against the heavy wrought-iron gate, which slowly swung inward. Pausing for a moment, he looked around.

Rows of tombs of all shapes and sizes stretched out before him. To his left stood a statue of a young woman, hands folded upon her knees, eyes gazing up to heaven. All around her stood other monuments: most in white marble, many crowned by a crucifix made of stone. There were also small houses made of stone, and some scattered trees.

José picked his way through the tombs, small and large, then past a fountain shooting water high in the air. A mound of flowers caught his attention, and he stopped. The swaths of carnations, orchids, and roses still gave off a beautiful aroma. On a small wooden plaque he could read the name: Anacleto Gonzàlez Flores.

A week earlier José heard the story of this hero from his uncle. The family had finished their after-dinner Rosary when the priest began, "I'm going to tell you about one of my good friends, Anacleto Gonzàlez Flores. He was a top-notch lawyer—the best in Guadalajara.

"When they closed the churches last July, he organized boycotts and tried to put pressure on the government to restore freedom of religion. But his attempts failed. When he offered to help the Cristeros, he instantly became a hunted man. In almost no time, the police raided the house where he was staying and put him in jail."

"Why, Padre Ignacio?" asked José. "Why did they put him in jail?"

"Oh, mainly because he was helping the Cristeros, but also because he knew where the Archbishop of Guadalajara was hiding. He refused to tell them. So they tortured and whipped him. He wouldn't speak. So they started to stab him."

José grimaced, as did the other members of the family.

"When the police stopped their torture," the priest continued, "Anacleto wrote, 'Viva Cristo Rey' on the wall of the jail with his own blood.

"His last words were: 'I die, but God does not die. Viva Cristo Rey.'"

Then and there, José resolved to visit the martyr's grave. Now, laying a hand against his plaque, he slipped to his knees and whispered, "Anacleto, I know you're in heaven because you died for Jesus. You had a lot of courage. I want to fight for God too, but I'm scared. The next time you talk to Jesus, please put in a good word for me. Tell him that I want to get to heaven to be with him. You, who are so close to God, please ask this grace for me."

He knelt in silence. Then, rising to his feet, he headed resolutely toward the gate.

That night, as the Sánchez del Río family sat around the dinner table, José waited for the right moment to speak. Doña Mariquita sat with the three girls at one end of the long rectangular table, and Don Macario was at the other end with him and Guillermo. Next to José lay two untouched plates before two empty chairs. They belonged to Macario and Miguel.

Shortly after they had left home to join the Cristeros, the family received a terse message saying that they had made it safely to the camp and been accepted into the army. As far as the family knew, they were both still alive and well. *Will I be so lucky*, wondered José.

In the center of the table sat a large basket of steaming tortillas. A platter of chicken slowly made its way from person to person. After serving himself some, José ladled some *pico de gallo* on top. Pico de gallo— diced tomatoes, cilantro, onions, freshly squeezed lime juice, and peppers—was his favorite salsa; it tasted good on most everything. He took one bite and relished the explosion of flavor in silence. As always, Doña Mariquita's food was so scrumptious that words weren't necessary.

That's one of the things that keeps our family together, he thought, a grin spreading across his face, *Mamà and her food. I doubt the Cristeros eat as well as we do.*

Only the noise of forks and knives could be heard. The whole family was eating their meal with gusto. Looking around the table at his family, Jose thought, *I'm going to miss them. Now that I'm ready to ask, I don't want to leave any of them. I wish I could take them with me.*

With the main course over, Doña Mariquita went to the kitchen. She returned carrying a squat amber custard with dark-brown syrup oozing down the sides.

"Flan!" squealed Celia.

After the plates had been scoured of every drop of caramel sauce, Don Macario stood up and led the family into the living room. As they passed Doña Mariquita, she handed out rosaries from a wooden cabinet.

Each member of the family had a role in leading some of the prayers of the Rosary, and afterward, Doña Mariquita and her three daughters cleared the table and washed the dishes while José and his older brother Guillermo stayed in the living room with their father. Don Macario sat down in his big armchair and pulled out a book. José stood in the opposite corner fumbling with his hands. *How should I say it?* he asked himself. *Is this the right moment?* His heart beat quicker. *If I don't ask now, I never will.*

"Papá," he said, drawing near his father. "May I ask you an important question?"

Don Macario took off his reading glasses and turned toward his son. "What's on your mind?" he asked, smiling.

José fidgeted a little and swallowed.

"Go on, son. I'm listening."

"Um, well, you know how Macario and Miguel went off to join the Cristeros? Well, . . . uh . . . I want to be a Cristero too."

Don Macario didn't say anything. Setting down the book, he closed his eyes for a moment and drew his hands together. Wrinkles spread across his brow. He stroked his short white beard. Then he opened his eyes again and gazed at his son before beginning to speak.

"José, your desire is very noble. God knows that the Cristeros are our only hope for peace and freedom now." He paused, and then spread wide his hands.

"But you're only fourteen. I wonder if any Cristero general would accept you."

Doña Mariquita had come from the kitchen and was standing beside her husband.

"Maybe if you wait till you are older—maybe then you can be a Cristero," his father continued. "I just don't see it happening now."

José leaned closer to his father. "I thought the same thing too, Papá. But today I was praying at Anacleto's tomb, and I felt that now is the moment. Winning heaven has never been so easy. Now's my chance. I don't think I'll have another like it."

Doña Mariquita and Don Macario looked at each other.

Inside, José struggled. *I wish I had been born ten years earlier.*

Don Macario coughed a little. He nodded his head at Doña Mariquita and then turned again to José.

"José, guessing that you would someday be asking us this question, your mother and I already decided this matter. For us, there is nothing more important than God and his rights. The truth is, we support the Cristeros in as many ways as we can—more than you know. But we can't just let you run off to join the army —not at your age anyway."

I knew it, whispered a little voice inside José. *I should not have even asked.*

Don Macario wasn't finished. "That's why we've decided that if a Cristero general accepts you, you can have our blessing."

∼

First thing in the morning, José began writing his letter to General Ignacio Sánchez Ramírez. He strained against the paper as he tried to recall his teacher's instructions from handwriting class: "Dot your i's and cross your t's. Straight lines. Full sentences. Capitalize the first words. Don't forget your accents." After seven false starts, seven crumpled sheets littered the floor. Pleased with his eighth try, he gingerly laid down the pen and admired his masterpiece.

General Ignacio Sánchez Ramírez

Dear General Ramírez,

My name is José Sánchez del Río. I am fourteen and live in Sahuayo. My brothers Marcario and Miguel are Cristeros, and I want to be one too.

If I am not old enough to handle a gun, I may be helpful in other ways, such as saddling the horses or carrying water and ammunition. And besides that, I could help with the cooking.

I'll do whatever you need me to, just please, may I join your army?

Yours truly,
José Sánchez del Río

Looks good to me, José thought. He carefully folded the letter and slipped it into an envelope. *Now to find someone to deliver it.*

As he headed downstairs, a delightful aroma caught his nose. His feet instinctively followed the fragrance to its source.

"Fresh *pan dulce,*" he murmured as he strode into the kitchen. His mother was pulling a sheet of small pink and yellow buns from the oven. José felt his stomach growl. Summing up all the sweetness he could, he said, "Mamá, do you think I could maybe have one pan dulce, please?"

Doña Mariquita eyed her boy. *This one sure has a knack for appearing at the perfect moment*, she thought. "Where have you been hiding all this time?" she asked with a smile.

The letter in José's hand slipped back into his memory. "Oh, um, . . . I was writing to General Ramírez, and—" He paused as he saw his mother's face fall.

"You and Papá said it was OK if I try to get accepted, remember?" José clutched the letter tightly and barreled on. "Well, I need someone to deliver my letter to the Cristeros."

He studied his mother's face, saw the tears forming in her eyes. *She doesn't want me to go. I might as well give up now.*

"Mamá . . ." his voice trailed off. He stepped forward with arms outstretched. She set down the hot tray and hugged him tightly. Then Doña Mariquita grabbed José's shoulders and looked straight at him through her teary eyes.

"*Hijito mío*," she said, "I don't want to lose you." She hugged him again and ran one hand through his springy black hair. "I wish this war never happened." Leaning her head back, she wiped the tears first from one eye, then from the other. After sniffling a bit, she continued, "No, you can't have any pan dulce."

José looked longingly at the sweet buns and then back

at his mother, who smiled and said, "I made them for the Cristeros. I'm taking them and some other food to their camp this afternoon. We can hide your letter in the basket."

José handed her his letter, and his mother handed back a bun. "*Muchas gracias*, Mamá," he said and gave her a kiss on the cheek.

Full of hopeful excitement, José ran to the small stables behind the house. As he opened one of the doors, it squeaked on its rusty hinges, and immediately a loud neigh sounded from within.

"Don't worry, Copper; it's me, José." The boy shut the door behind him and strode over to the chestnut horse that was his prized possession. He had raised it from a foal, and now that the animal was full grown, he rode it whenever he could.

Holding up his hand, José offered the animal a slice of apple. Copper took a sniff, and then the fruit was gone.

José laughed. "You old magician, how do you do that without biting my hand off?"

Copper chomped away at the apple contentedly.

Pulling a brush from the wall, José stroked the horse's sides, combing out brambles.

"Copper, guess what? All this time I thought Mamá had been spending her afternoons over at the Espinosas' house. She always disappeared after lunch and wouldn't come home until dinner.

"But that was for show. She's really been secretly delivering food and supplies to the Cristeros. She takes turns with other ladies in the town. No one in the government suspects them yet. She's going to take my letter to General Ramírez today."

The horse didn't show much interest in José's tale. Instead, it was sniffing at one of his pockets.

"Silly horse. Pan dulce is bad for you. Mamá gave me one because she said it's to make up for all the sweets I'll miss if the Cristeros really do accept me. You'll need a lot of apples to make up for all the ones you'll miss too. We'll be going together."

Copper neighed softly.

"Let's see," said José. "I've got a horse. I think I have the clothes I need." He paused.

Copper whinnied.

"You're right," said José, grinning and giving the horse a pat. "All that's missing is a gun."

MAPA DE SAHUAYO, MICH.

VIVA CRISTO REY

5

PREPARATIONS

THUD, THUD, THUD. Doña Mariquita looked up from the book she was reading and listened. *Thud, thud, thud.* There it was again. Someone must be knocking gently but firmly on the front door, she realized.

She got to her feet and made her way down the hall.

"Who's there?" she asked, ear to the door.

"It's me," said a voice. "Trino."

She undid the latch, and the door swung inward. "Looking for José?"

The boy swept the sombrero off his head and gave a little bow.

"Sí, Señora. Do you know where he is?"

"He went to the courtyard after lunch," she said sadly. "He didn't like the general's answer."

"*Caramba*," said Trino.

Doña Mariquita smiled and started down the hallway. "He must be with Copper. That horse has to be the most beloved animal in all of Sahuayo."

Trino nodded and followed after her.

Opening the door to the courtyard, she gave a look around. "José, Trino's here," she called.

"Go ahead, Trino," said Doña Mariquita. "*Merienda* is at five."

"Gracias," said Trino, who found José brushing down his horse. "I heard the news," Trino said, as Copper sniffed at him.

José didn't look up and didn't answer.

"Is it that bad?"

José nodded.

"The general said you can't go?"

"Sí" was the terse reply. The chestnut horse snorted.

"Wait a minute, José. What did the letter actually say?"

"General Ramírez thinks that I would serve the Cristeros better by staying at home and doing nothing."

"Hmm . . . didn't he say anything else? Didn't he give you any options?"

"Not that I saw," replied José, setting the brush

down. "Although I was so angry when I read the first line that—"

"That you didn't read the whole thing?" finished Trino, stepping forward and laying a hand on the horse's side.

José shrugged his shoulders. "What use is there?" he asked. "I have my answer. I ripped the thing to pieces."

"As long as you still have the pieces we can put the letter back together—you know, like a jigsaw puzzle."

"If you say so," replied José.

"Of course I do. *Vámonos.*"

The boys went to Jose's room and began piecing together the general's torn up letter.

"Here's his signature, big and flowery," said Jose.

"So these pieces go at the bottom," said Trino. "And here's your name—top left corner."

Soon José was able to read aloud:

Dear José,

While I appreciate your offer of help, I think it better that you wait until you are older to join my regiment.

I doubt that any general would be willing to receive you at such a young age, especially here in the Sahuayo district.

Ramírez

"*Especially here in the Sahuayo district,*" both boys repeated together.

"José, do you know what this means?"

"That I should have read it more carefully," said the boy, shaking his head.

"You—I mean, *we*—don't have to limit ourselves to the Sahuayo district," Trino explained. "You have a horse, right?"

José nodded, a large smile spreading across his face. "Now that you mention it, I remember Papá talking about some Cristeros down by Cotija. Maybe we could join up with them."

~

That evening after the family Rosary, José asked his parents if he could join the Cristeros near Cotija. They left the room for a moment to discuss it privately, and when they returned Don Macario said, "José, your mother and I realize that your desire to be a Cristero soldier is a noble thing." He paused and glanced at his wife before continuing. "But we still think you're too young to be fighting in battles."

Here it comes, thought José. *They're going to insist on my having written permission.*

"That's why," Don Macario coughed, looked at Doña Mariquita, and continued, "that's why we have decided to let you go under one condition."

José's face lit up. "Condition? Sure—anything. What is it?"

"We don't want you fighting until you've turned sixteen. So you can go, not as a soldier, but as a helper."

The smile on José's face shifted to a look of puzzlement.

"Do you think they'll still want me?" he asked. "The Cristeros need *soldiers*."

Laying a hand on José's knee, Doña Mariquita spoke, "They need all the help they can get—not just in the fighting. There's all the food to cook, horses to take care of, equipment that needs cleaning—there's plenty to do."

Don Macario nodded. "If they don't want you, you are to come back home immediately."

"Sí, Papá," said the boy, eyes wide with wonder.

Doña Mariquita spoke again. "José, I know I've told you this before, but your father and I are only looking out for your good. We believe this is what's best for you."

He smiled and stretched out his arms, wrapping them both in a big hug. "All right," he said, squeezing hard. "When can I start?"

"First, visit your Tía Magdalena," said Doña Mariquita. "She will tell you what to do."

~

"Your mamá and papá really said you may go?"

José sat in the living room of his aunt's house.

"That's what I was telling you, Tía Magdalena. Don't you believe me?"

"Of course I do, José. I just thought you might be trying to pull my leg."

"Not this time. I came to you because I need some advice."

The tall lady straightened up in her chair. "Don't get me wrong, José. It's not that I don't think you can help the Cristeros—and they certainly need all the help they can get; God knows that. It's just—you're so young. I bring them supplies almost every day, and I haven't met anyone your age there."

"But those are the Cristeros of Sahuayo," said José. "I want to go to Cotija. Anyway, the worst thing they could say is no. What's there to lose?"

"Do you think they'll accept you?"

José shrugged his shoulders. "I'm not sure, but I just have to try. It's my only chance. If I don't go and help now, we might never get the churches open again."

The boy sure has his heart set on this, she thought.

"All right, I'll help."

"Thank you, Tía Magdalena!" said José, jumping from his seat to embrace his aunt.

"First things first," said his aunt. "Do you know how to get to Cotija?" José shook his head. "It can't be that hard, Tía Magdalena. If I get lost, I follow the signs, right?"

José's aunt let out a long sigh. "Men—you're all the same. Always think you know the way, until you're utterly lost." She tossed her arms in the air and pointed a finger at her nephew. "Don't expect there to be signs anywhere. You, my little friend, are going to need a map."

"I'm not afraid of asking for directions."

"The first thing you should be wary of," she warned him, "is talking to strangers. Anyone who wanders about these days probably isn't up to any good. And you can't count on your luck to get you anywhere."

"So I need a map," José ceded. "What else?"

"You'll need enough food to last you the whole journey, because you can't count on finding much along the way." She thought a little. "Then there's water— you'll need some canteens. You'll need something to sleep under—"

"Like the clothes on my back," José blurted out.

"Or so you think, until you get up into the mountains, and you wake up one morning covered in rain or frozen-stiff like a block of ice."

"Really?" asked José.

"Really. The Cristeros have told me." She took her nephew by the shoulders and stared into his eyes. "You, my dear nephew, are a city-boy. You have many things to learn—like how to build a fire. Add a flint to your list."

José scribbled on a wrinkled sheet of paper and then said, "A map, food for me and Copper, canteens for water, blankets, a piece of flint . . . anything else?"

Aunt Magdalena shook her head. "That's all I can think of now. Better get to work."

"But how?" asked José. "I only have a few *centavos*, and most of the stores are closed now anyway."

"Let me see that list."

José handed her the slip of paper.

"Hmm," she said, running her eyes up and down. "A map I can get. Food, you can find. A canteen— you'll have to buy that. I have a few spare blankets. Flint? Why don't you ask Chema?"

"Because I just gave Chema my last peso to buy my gun."

"Well, you'll have to find some more pesos. Maybe you can do some chores."

She paused and wiped her glasses with her apron. Then turning back to José, she added, "And come to think of it, you'll need to learn how to cook. Tía María can teach you that. Otherwise, you might spend all your time shoveling manure."

∼

"Hey, careful, you're dripping on me."

"Whose idea was this anyway? I was all for going straight to Cotija."

"It was my tía Magdalena's idea, and she's pretty smart," said José, grinning, as he slapped a large swath of paint on the wall.

Trino paused, looking down from the top of the ladder at José, who stood on the bottom rung. "How many of these odd jobs do we have to do?" he asked.

"Oh, I don't know," replied José, chuckling. "As much as it takes to buy all our supplies."

"I'd give anything to play *fútbol* right now," Trino said.

"Me too," José agreed, continuing to paint. "But we are so close to our goal, I don't want to stop for anything. Let's see, we've swept my house and your house and Tía Magdalena's house. We cleaned out too many chicken coops—yuck. We picked up those pine cones. We sold my bottle cap collection—"

"And Nacho," interrupted Trino.

"And Nacho, your turtle," acknowledged José, "who would *not* have made a good Cristero."

Trino dipped his brush in the bucket.

José continued, "All in all, I like the painting most. I figure we'll have enough money by next Friday. Then we'll go to Cotija!"

"One more week," said Trino, swishing his brush against the wall. "I don't know if I can make it that long."

"Sure you will," said José. "We'll be leaving before you know it. All we've got to do is finish this painting, and my tía Magdalena will do the rest. She's the best."

"You're right about that," said a voice from behind.

The two boys turned around, sprinkling the floor with paint as they did.

"Tía Magdalena," José asked excitedly, "what brings you our way?"

Ignoring the question, she pointed at José. "For heaven's sake young man, what is that in your hands?" she asked.

José smiled. "It's a better paint brush," he said. "I took an old broom and tied three paint brushes to it —three is faster than one."

"If there wasn't more paint on the ground than on the wall," said Aunt Magdalena, hands on her hips, "I might call you intelligent."

"Uh oh," said José.

"Well, I didn't come to scold you." Sticking a hand in her satchel, she pulled out a wrinkled, weather-stained sheet of paper.

"I've got your map."

José winked at Trino. "How did you do it?" he asked.

"I forced those Cristeros to make it. I told the chef's assistant that he could say good-bye to his fresh meat and vegetables if he didn't find me someone to make a map. That did the trick. General Ramírez himself drew this. He's the only one that knows the area well enough."

"You mean *the* General Ramírez, the one who won't accept me into his army?" asked José.

"A hungry man will do just about anything for food."

Trino and José laughed. Tía Magdalena smiled and

added, "That reminds me. You have to learn how to cook before you go. Tía María sent me here to get you. You can learn *frijoles, carne asada, maíz*—you know—the basics. You may be too young to fight, but not to do kitchen work."

"It's a shame," added Trino, reaching down for more paint.

Later that night, Don Macario sat with his son after dinner.

"Gosh," said José, rubbing his left hand. "Tía María is pretty tough for an old lady."

"I wouldn't call her old," suggested Don Macario. "After all, she's my little sister."

"Well, she made it all look so easy: 'First you get your fire lit. Then you put the beans in the kettle. Make sure to stir the beans as they cook.' She grabbed the kettle with her bare hand. When I tried, the handle almost cooked my skin off—that's Tía for you."

"A little burn won't hurt you," said Don Macario, leaning over to look at José's palm. "You put some aloe on it, right?"

"Mamá did, but it still hurts."

"You'll need to be able to take a lot more than that if you want to be a Cristero, José."

"You're probably right."

"What's this map you were talking about?" asked Don Macario, changing the subject.

"Oh, yeah," answered José, pulling the piece of paper from his pocket.

Don Macario whistled. "Excellent," he said, eyes glued to the map. "Whoever made this sure knew his geography."

"Tía Magdalena says that General Ramírez made it. She forced him to."

"Tía Magdalena forced General Ramírez?" asked Don Macario.

"She threatened to stop bringing food."

"Ha, ha. Sounds like my little sister. Say, José, I've been meaning to give you something. Wait here a minute."

José studied the map while he waited for his father. Though handwritten, it was packed with detail. In the northwest was the large outline of Lake Chapala, and next to that lay Sahuayo. Cotija sat toward the bottom of the sheet. Between the two towns a few lines indicated country roads. These were crisscrossed by thicker squiggly lines—mountains, wild land where no one lived.

Don Macario walked back into the room. In his hand he held a small, bronze-colored container. "I haven't used this since my days on the ranch," he said, rubbing his fingers across the weathered surface of the object. "My father gave it to me, so I guess it's fitting that I give it to you."

He slipped off the metal lid of the small container. Inside, a needle floated, suspended on a point.

"This is a treasure," said Don Macario as he carefully placed it in José's hands. "They don't make them like this anymore. If you know where north is, you're never lost."

"Wow," said José, goggle-eyed. "For me?"

"You need it more than I do," replied Don Macario, reaching over and picking up the sheet of paper. "Let's go over this map. You'll have to learn how to use the compass properly before you go anywhere."

José nodded in agreement.

"As far as which route to take, I think fastest is best. Once you leave Sahuayo, you can skirt Jiquilpan and then follow the main road west. If you go under cover of night, the road should be clear. Just follow the signs to Quitupan."

"Wouldn't it be quicker to cut across the countryside and make straight for Cotija?" asked José.

"If these were plains, sure," explained Don Macario waving his hand across the bottom part of the map. "The problem is, you'd be heading straight through mountains. Who knows what you'll run into? Roads are the only safe way, especially at night."

"Well, I hope I can find my way in the dark," said José, head bent over the map.

"That's where the compass comes in handy. If you follow the contours of these hills—they are actually very detailed here—and if you use your compass faithfully, you can't miss the turns. Take the first right, then the second left after that, and soon you'll be in Quitupan. There's a regiment of federal soldiers stationed there, so you'll do best to keep low."

"And after I get to Quitupan, I head south through the hills, right?"

"Not hills—mountains. This one here, Cerro San Francisco, is over eight thousand feet high."

"Wow, that *is* high."

"You'll take a left in the town square in Quitupan—everyone will be asleep—and then the road will take you along the base of these cliffs." Here he pointed to a row of narrow lines.

"After the hills let up, you'll come alongside Laguna de San Juanico. If you skirt the lake from the south, you can't miss Cotija. It's not as big as Sahuayo, but still, it's a town. Where are you supposed to meet the Cristeros?"

"Tía Magdalena said they'd be in the mountains south of town. She said there are so many Cristeros there I'm bound to find my way to the general, if they don't mistake me for a spy and spear me first."

Don Macario looked skeptical. "They're not that stupid."

"I figure that if I make it to Cotija in one piece, then I've done pretty well," said José.

"Oh, I'm sure you'll make it there just fine," said Don Macario, yawning and glancing at his pocket watch. "It's past my bedtime now—and yours. Good night, young man."

6

PICAZO

IN HIS ROOMY CORNER OFFICE on the town square, Rafael Picazo paced back and forth. As he walked, he stroked his shiny black handlebar moustache methodically.

The desk by the window was nearly as neat as the moustache. Made from mahogany, it was rich-looking, sturdy, and formidable. It made him feel powerful to sit behind it in his tall executive chair and receive people who came to him with their problems.

Being mayor of a town like Sahuayo wasn't normally an exalted position, but war had changed that. Rafael Picazo now had broad powers, if he chose to use them —even life-and-death power over every inhabitant of the town.

But Picazo was worried too. As he smoothed the left tip of his shiny moustache, his eyes strayed again to the typewritten title of the secret government document on his desk: "Known Cristero Locations". According to the report, Sahuayo was basically surrounded by roving bands of Cristeros. None stayed too long in any one place, but the vast majority of them seemed to be hiding in and around the mountains south and east of town. *Just my luck*, Picazo said to himself.

The mayor had thought that after he and his cronies stormed—and took—the town churches, all his problems would be settled. The federal soldiers with their cannon had certainly made a big impression on the people. But the cannons were gone now, bringing "peace" to some other town. For the time being, Sahuayo and his rule over it were in a weakened position.

His rule over his own family was also on shaky ground. Ever since the shootout at the Church of Santiago, his wife had barely spoken to him. "But Rafael," she had said at the time, "it's as if you've sold your soul away. You know deep down that what you did was wrong, don't you? An innocent boy was killed, a holy priest was seriously wounded, and God's house was desecrated."

"Consuelo, I'm an employee of the government," he had answered. "Orders are orders, and they ordered me to take over the churches. If I had disobeyed, I would've lost my position and the children would have nothing to eat."

"Rafael, to tell you the truth, I'd rather the children go hungry than have their father destroy himself. You used to bring the children to Mass with me, pray the Rosary with us . . . I no longer know the man I married."

"Last time I checked," he had said with a snarl, "I was still the head of this household. Your job is to take care of the children. My job is to make a living."

Picazo had never before spoken to his wife so harshly, and he soon regretted it, especially since he doubted the government's policy against the Church and suspected that his wife was probably right.

But that was then. Now that the Cristeros were engaged in open war against the government, he felt certain that his duty was to defend it.

Ambling over to the far corner of the room, he stopped before a cabinet with an oval mirror. He eyed his reflection and nudged the left side of his moustache a little higher, balancing it out. *But the Cristeros are gaining strength*, his reflection seemed to say. *Are you fighting for a lost cause?*

"No," he said out loud, "this is a noble cause. I am fighting to preserve law and order from these vigilantes and their version of justice."

He fumbled with one of the cabinet drawers. Inside sat a box of cigars. The enticing smell of tobacco drifted up. He drew out a cigar and strolled back to his desk, where another document drew his attention: "Known Cristeros". He sat down and leafed through the ten pages of names. Many were underlined in red ink.

"My own people—traitors." He spat into the trash can at his feet.

He had already set the pages back down, when a strange idea struck him. Picking the document up again, he studied the names written in red: Guízar, Galvez, Hurtado, Castañeda, Ochoa, Lopez . . . With each turn of the page, a slight grin began to worm its way across his moustached face. From time to time, his eyebrows raised a little.

When he had finished his survey, he laid the document down and let out a short laugh. "So stupid, these people. Ha! Stupid . . . and rich."

7

THE JOURNEY

T HE TIPS OF THE SOLITARY HEDGE shone emerald
green in the rays of the dying sun. Sahuayo had
seen its fair share of gorgeous weather the whole month
of June. Cool nights had been followed by pleas-
antly warm days with crystal-clear skies. Now a breeze
tugged at the trees and the bushes.

The hedge shook a little as a cloak-draped figure
poked his head through a gap in the leaves. In his left
hand were the reins of a horse. The figure stood still

64

for a moment, surveying the surrounding plain. All was
clear. The only movement came from the swallows that
dipped and plunged through the air overhead.

"Where's Trino?" José asked his horse.

Turning, he peeked into the bundle on Copper's
back. His canteen, Trino's, their blankets, food, the
map—everything was just as he had packed it. The
two revolvers lay well hidden at the bottom.

The horse whinnied, giving José a start.

"Easy boy, he'll be here soon."

Just then a rustling came from the hedge, and José
turned in time to see a head peek through.

"Is the coast clear?" Trino whispered.

"What took you so long?" asked José impatiently.

"I was saying good-bye," said Trino, pulling himself
through the hedge.

By now the gray dusk had begun its slow advance
across the plain. In the southwest, just above the mountain tops, a vivid red filled the sky.

"I hope your horse can see well in the dark," said
Trino.

"Oh, I'm hoping we don't reach the tricky part till
sunrise," answered José.

Slipping his foot into a stirrup, he gave a soft grunt as
he lifted himself up into the saddle. Turning to Trino,
he leaned over and gave him a hand up.

"Tough saying good-bye?" asked José, once they
were both seated atop the horse.

Trino nodded. "Sí."

"Me too," said José. "Felt like I was leaving my heart behind." He swallowed and then squeezed the reins. "No matter. Ready?"

"All set," said Trino, managing a grin.

"All right then," said José. He bent down to Copper's ear. "OK, buddy, now's your chance. We have to get to Cotija by tomorrow afternoon. Thirty miles —you can do it."

Copper needed no whip. He cantered off in the direction José pointed.

As the horse made its way across the plains toward the hills, José turned and watched Sahuayo growing smaller behind them.

~

"You sure?"

"Look, my papá said second left."

Skirting the town of Jiquilpan had been easy. The last light of dusk was just enough for them to make their way without being seen. Now they advanced by the light of a waxing moon.

"But where's the sign for Quitupan?"

"I don't know—never been there. But this has got to be it. All those other roads we passed looked like mule paths compared to this one," said José.

He pulled the reins to the left. Copper continued forward a little, as if he didn't want to turn. José kept pulling until the horse reluctantly swung its head to the side.

Unlike the main road, here trees drooped over them, casting shadows on the already scant light.

"I hope Copper can see better than I can in this darkness," said José.

"I don't have a good feeling about this," Trino said nervously.

José noticed movement ahead. He straightened up in the saddle and leaned forward to get a better view. Just then, a tree branch whacked him in the forehead, and he tumbled off the horse.

Trino grabbed at the saddle, barely managing to stay atop the horse, and Copper came to a halt.

"José, are you all right?"

A weak voice came from the darkness below. "I don't know."

Trino dismounted and helped José to his feet. Feeling his forehead, José could tell a lump was forming, but he wasn't bleeding.

"It's just a bump," said José. "Why don't we . . . uh . . . why don't we go back to the main road?"

"Good idea," said Trino.

José grabbed the loose reins and added, "I think I'll walk Copper back, just to be on the safe side."

A couple of miles down the main road they came across the sign for Quitupan.

"Told you so."

"I know, I know. I've got the bump, remember?"

"It's your first battle scar," said Trino.

"Now you're talking. We can say that we were way-laid by bandits, and I fought them off bravely," said José, guiding Copper to the left.

"And that you woke up from your dream when a branch whacked you," said Trino, chuckling.

A hush accompanied the darkness all around them. Neither beast nor man stirred on the dusty road to Quitupan. Mile after mile they trotted along in silence.

Then, ever so slowly, the path grew clearer again. A faint light came from behind them, in the east. The sound of birds chirping reached their ears. Soon the color on the leaves started to return, faint at first, and then steadily building with every twist and turn they took. Heading round a curve between two eroded cliff walls, a few feeble rays of sunlight struck their faces.

Ridges and valleys riddled the country here. A light fog huddled in the low spots, and when they came to the top of a hill, they could spy an endless procession of wooded ridges thrusting up through the mist. Here and there a grove of pines reared its head up as if in defiance of the smaller trees. Besides these little erup-tions of branches, the land was covered with a uniform carpet of green.

Crossing over a small stream, they approached a wall of fog.

"I don't like the look of this," said José.

"Fog's better than darkness," said Trino.

"If you say so."

Copper plunged in. Seconds later, Trino couldn't see more than ten feet away in any direction.

Fortunately, the trampled mud and grass of the road stood out clearly from the surrounding fields.

The horse didn't need any guiding. It followed the twists and turns just as well as the straight parts. José let the reins droop low.

As they rounded a wide bend, a soft ringing of bells came drifting over the wind. José pulled Copper to a halt and listened, peering through the fog.

"I'll bet there are cows nearby. Can't mistake that smell," he said.

"If there are cows, there's bound to be a farm too," said Trino. "I'm thirsty. Maybe we can borrow some milk."

"Borrow? I kind of doubt we'd ever give it back."

"You know what I mean, said Trino, shaking his head. "I'm going to ask for some milk. You can stay here if you want."

"We must stick together, Trino. If you're that thirsty, let's find the farm."

José flicked the reins and steered Copper in the direction of the bells. Soon a fence emerged from the fog, and they followed alongside it. Just ahead, a dark shape loomed up.

"Looks like a farmhouse," said José.

"Whatever happens, be careful," said Trino. "We don't want to blow our cover before we meet the

Cristeros. I'm Pancho and you're Pepe, and we're going to Cotija to help Grandpa plant the crops."

José nodded.

They could now see the whitewashed walls of a building. The only door in sight was open, and light streamed from within.

"Let me do the talking," said Trino, as he slipped off the horse's back and landed on the ground.

José jumped down after his friend and led Copper by the reins.

Instead of approaching the open door, Trino positioned himself at the foot of the porch steps and rapped on the house with his knuckles. There was silence. After a moment, he knocked again and gave a loud "Anybody home?"

A noise came from their right, and both boys turned to see the back of a tall, skinny man dressed in a tattered gray cloak. He was pulling on a rope, which, they soon saw, was tied around the neck of a donkey. Strapped atop the donkey was a towering stack of rifles.

When the man had drawn up close, he stopped pulling, turned, and saw the boys. He looked them up and down and then spat to the side—tobacco juice.

"Good morning, strangers," he said, lifting his hat. "I'm Señor Chávez."

Thump, thump, thump went José's heart. The bridle trembled in his hands. "Uh . . . ," he began, trailing off.

"I'm Pancho," said Trino, stepping forward.

"Uh . . . and I am too," said José. A sharp jab between his shoulder blades made him wince. "I mean . . . I'm here with Pancho. My name's Pepe."

"We're . . . uh . . . we're trying to find Cotija, and we were looking for some milk," said Trino.

"Milk I have," said the man, eyebrows raised quizzically. "But it's awful strange to find two youngsters on the road at this hour. Might I ask your business?"

"We're going to Cotija . . . ," began Trino. "We're going to Cotija to help plant crops—"

"—Cristeros," blurted José.

Another sharp jab. This time José gave a yelp.

"You two all right?" asked the man, head cocked to the side. "My wife tells me I'm losing my hearing, but . . . you say you're going to Cotija to plant *Cristeros*?"

"To become Cristeros," said José, stepping forward. "I'm José, and this is Trino, and we're going to Cotija to join the Cristeros—if they'll have us."

"My, my," said the old man, scratching his white hair.

"And we'd like something to drink."

At this, the man nodded. "All right then, follow me," he said, turning around and towing the donkey behind him.

"I'm going to *kill* you," muttered Trino beneath his breath.

José waved a hand.

After tying up the donkey, the man turned and said, "Give me a moment to let my wife know we've got company."

He stepped inside.

"Now what?" asked Trino, throwing his arms up.

"What do you mean?" replied José, staring at the pile of weapons. "Are you scared?"

"If I'm here, it means I'm not scared. I just don't think—"

Señor Chávez came striding out the door and onto the porch. Leaning over the railing, he spat into a bucket and waved them over.

"Come on in. You boys need breakfast? My wife says you're welcome to a bite if you'd like."

José laid a hand on his stomach and smiled. Then he bounded up the steps to the house. He stopped before the doorway, turning. "What about my horse? He'll be hungry too," he asked.

"I could give him a little something to eat, if you want," said the man. "Appears he's traveled a lot recently."

Trino nodded as he picked up the reins José had dropped and handed them over.

"You two run along to the kitchen while I take care of these good creatures," said the old man as he led Copper to where the donkey stood tethered.

Trino gingerly made his way up the steps and through the open doorway. José had already stepped inside. Trino paused, hesitating on the threshold, half expecting to see a potato sack drop over his friend's head. But nothing happened, so he plunged into the house as well.

Señora Chávez greeted the two boys warmly and led them to a rough wooden table in the kitchen. When her husband walked in from tending to the animals, they were up to their necks in fresh bread, jam, and milk.

"So where are you two from?" asked Señor Chávez.

"Sahuayo," said José, as he slathered creamy yellow butter onto a slice of freshly baked bread.

"We left last night."

"It was awful dark most of the way," said Trino.

"That was because you were staring at my back," said José.

Ignoring the remark, Trino continued. "We almost got lost too. If it hadn't been for my bravery—"

"Ahem, *bravery*?" interrupted José.

Trino took another swig from a glass of frothy milk. "Call it what you like, I did find the right road," he said, licking his lips.

"There *is* some truth to that," José admitted.

Señora Chávez brought to the table a steaming platter of *chilaquiles*: tortilla chips with pulled chicken smothered in salsa, sour cream, refried beans and crumbled cheese.

Both boys piled their plates high. Trino cocked his head and gave José a triumphant look.

"So, you're headed to Cotija?" asked Señor Chávez.

José was in the middle of twisting and inserting a heavily laden fork sideways into his mouth, and it barely fit. Still chewing, he attempted a feeble response. "Buhh" was all he could say.

Trino's cheeks bulged as he attempted to gulp down the chilaquiles. The *jalapeño* salsa was so hot, huge drops of sweat bathed his face.

José cleared his windpipe enough to speak, and answered, "Sí. We're going to join the Cristeros."

Trino didn't protest the revelation this time, intent as he was on his plate.

Señora Chávez, who had finished cleaning up from her cooking, sat down across from José. "Aren't you boys a little young to be doing something like that?" she asked.

Setting down his breakfast-laden fork, José answered, "Yes, that's what most people say. And it's not like we've been accepted into the Cristero army yet. But it can't hurt to try, right? There are plenty of things we could do to help."

"Excuse me if I ask, but you didn't run away from home now, did you?" asked Señora Chávez.

Trino shook his head energetically. "No, no, no. My mamá and papá said I could go. I promise." He hastily jammed another overloaded fork into his mouth.

José spoke up, "My parents said I could go too. It was tough for them, but they have a lot of faith, my parents. After that, all we had to do was get our supplies together and figure out a route to Cotija. Which reminds me, how do you get to Cotija from here?"

"I'll show you the way, when you're ready," said Señor Chávez. "Just take your time now and finish that breakfast. You'll need your energy for the journey."

After they finished eating, the two yawning boys reluctantly accepted Señor Chávez's offer of a place to nap. By the time they awoke, cleaned up, and thanked Señora Chávez for breakfast, the sun was high in the sky.

"I'd say you'll reach Cotija by early afternoon," said Señor Chávez as the boys mounted Copper.

Pointing out some buildings in the distance, he said, "The quickest way is to pass through town and turn left. Then follow the road as it winds along the base of Cerro Torrecillas. If you take a wrong turn, you could end up lost in some remote mountain valley."

"Aren't there any signs?" asked Trino.

"Not that I remember," said Señor Chávez. "But there aren't many roads either, so it's hard to take a wrong turn."

"We've got a compass, so we can follow that south," said José.

"That might help. Once you come to Cotija, I suppose you know where to find your friends. Have a safe trip." He waved them on their way.

"You could have got us killed; that guy might be on the federal side," railed Trino once they were out of earshot.

"But I didn't. We're still alive, aren't we?"

"Alive for now. But we have to be extra careful."

"I think it was all worth it for that breakfast," said José, adjusting the reins. "Those chilaquiles sure were something."

"True," said Trino, straightening his hat. "And after last night's ride, I was so sore. Guess I'd better get used to horses."

José shrugged. "That's if the Cristeros accept us."

~

A golden sun was already sinking behind the hilltops when José and Trino finally made it around Cotija. They had decided not to risk cutting through the town.

Once past it, finding their way had been difficult.

"You mean the general didn't tell you *where* to meet up with his army?" Trino asked.

"He's not going to tell anybody the exact location of his troops," José replied. "My tía Magdalena said that once we're south of Cotija, the Cristeros will be in the mountains—pretty much all over the place."

"I sure hope we find them soon—seems like only coyotes would live in a place like this."

Just then, bayonets flashed in the setting sun.

Three men dressed in dark clothing dashed in front of Copper and pointed their rifles at the boys. All wore double bands of bullets crossed over their chests.

"Stop! Who lives?" demanded one of the men.

José pulled Copper to a halt and said, "Christ the King lives. Viva Cristo Rey."

"What is your business?" asked the man, lowering his weapon.

A sigh of relief escaped José's lips. "We're looking for the general. We . . . we want to be Cristeros."

"Give me your names, and where you are from," he said.

"I'm José Sánchez del Río, from Sahuayo."

"I'm José Trinidad Flores Espinosa, but they call me Trino."

"I don't care what they call you," barked the soldier. "We have no orders to accept boys into the army. How am I supposed to know you're not spies?"

"We're not, I promise. We can explain everything to the general," said José.

"Show me your credentials."

Both boys stared at each other in bewilderment.

"Credentials?" José asked.

"Yes, your documents."

"We don't have any . . . but my brothers Macario and Miguel are Cristeros in Sahuayo, and my mamá, Doña Mariquita, brings them food and supplies."

At this, the soldier glanced at his fellow soldiers. "You may be telling the truth, or you could be lying," he snapped. "Why should I let you pass?"

José straightened up in the saddle.

"Because I didn't come to play games; I came here to fight in the army of Christ the King," he declared.

The soldier grunted. Stepping aside, he drew another soldier—who limped as he walked—with him. They started talking quietly. The third man kept his rifle trained on the boys.

When they had finished, the soldier spoke again. "We'll let you pass, for now. You will follow Private Mijares here," he said, pointing to the soldier who limped. "But first, you must surrender any weapons you have."

José breathed a sigh of relief. He turned to Trino, who fished around in the bundle behind him until, with an "Aha," he drew out their two shiny pistols. These he handed to José, who passed them down to the officer.

"Do as Private Mijares says and speak clearly to the general," said the soldier. "And God go with you."

Mijares saluted the officer and hobbled his way over to a waiting horse. Once mounted, he beckoned to the boys, who followed him past the picket line. He kept an easy pace.

Darkness was now lengthening across the forest. José couldn't make out any path, though they seemed to be heading mainly uphill. It was just as well that they had someone to lead them.

Once over the brow of the first hill, they slipped silently down into a valley. Here a blanket of moss carpeted the ground, except for some places where leaves had piled up in small drifts. Across the valley's bottom ran a stream. When they reached it, the soldier led them to a shallow place where the horses could walk across.

Back in the forest, the trees cast inky shadows all around them.

"Who goes there?"

The words caught José off guard for there was no camp in sight. Another picket?

"Viva Cristo Rey. Private Mijares here. Lieutenant Gódinez sent me to bring these two boys to the general."

A lantern-beam splayed out across the three. "Oh, it's you, Mijares," said a voice. "Who did you say you brought with you?"

"Two boys who want to talk to the general."

"Are you certain of their identities?"

"Why don't you ask them?" said Private Mijares impatiently.

The soldier with the lantern didn't say anything as he looked the boys up and down.

"Explain yourselves," he said.

"I'm José, and this is Trino. We're from Sahuayo. We want to be Cristeros. We're looking for the general."

Noise came from the darkness behind the lantern. It was laughter. A smile appeared on the soldier's face.

"You know we have an age limit, don't you, son?" he asked.

José felt his forehead turning red.

"You have to be sixteen to fight. How old are you, ten? Why don't you go back home and take care of your mother?"

"Actually, I'm fourteen, and I didn't ask to fight. I just want to help. The general will understand—I am sure."

"I wouldn't be so sure about the general. It's not that I hold anything against you, son; it's just that facts are facts. The youngest man in the army right now is seventeen."

José bit his lip. *I'm not about to give up here*, he thought.

"I understand what you're saying," he told the soldier. "We are young. But we still want to try. The worst thing the general could do is send us back home." José paused before continuing. "If that's what he decides, . . . we'll do it."

In the dim light cast by the lantern, José saw the soldier rubbing his stubbly face. The lantern swung to the side for a moment as he glanced at those behind him.

Then facing the boys again, he sighed. "All right then. You still have to get past the third picket anyway, and García is a stickler. Good luck."

A little while later, the boys were stopped again. After the guard at the third picket heard their story he said, "I'm sorry, boys, but the general's got enough on his hands already. He can't spare time for the two of you."

José sat speechless atop his horse. *He can't turn us back after all this, not at the third picket,* he told himself.

"So you come from Sahuayo?" asked the guard.

"Yes, sir."

"And you left yesterday morning?"

"That's right."

"Where did you spend the night?"

"Near Quitupan. A family gave us breakfast and a place to sleep early this morning."

"Which family?"

"The Chávez family," replied José, as he fidgeted with the reins impatiently.

The soldier stiffened up. "Chávez! What?"

Before José could answer, the three sentries had stepped back, forming a tight knot. Every now and then a man would wave an arm in the boys' direction. One of them flagged Private Mijares, who joined in their discussion.

Baffled, José turned to Trino. "What did I say?"

Trino held up his hands in puzzlement. "Beats me."

After a heated discussion, the soldiers broke up and returned to their positions.

"Private Mijares will take you to headquarters now," barked the soldier in charge.

José shook his head in disbelief.

"And you'd better tell the general the whole story," growled the man.

One of the sentries stepped forward and quickly tied Copper to the saddle of Private Mijares' horse.

Trino shook José by the shoulder. "What's wrong?" he whispered.

"I have no idea," replied José, as Private Mijares started off.

Mijares led the boys at a snail's pace through the forest. Darkness seemed to fill the very gaps between their eyes. Eventually a steep hill rose up before them. The higher they went, the more the incline grew. Once over the brow of the hill, lights appeared in the distance. The horses paused a moment from their exertions.

Looking down, the boys could see a valley lit with many fires. They were shaped like two large circles meeting in the center.

"Follow me closely," said Private Mijares.

8

THE CRISTERO CAMP

A S THE BOYS began their descent toward the Cristero camp, the wind carried the sound of voices
to their ears. It wasn't shouting or singing, just quiet
voices rising and falling in the night.

Drawing nearer, they could make out the individ-
ual bonfires, each encircled by a ring of men. As they
approached the first fire, a hush fell, and many eyes
turned to face them. "That you, Mijares?" shouted
one of the men. "Shouldn't you be on picket duty?"

"Business for the general," he replied curtly.

They kept moving, zigzagging their way through the tents and fires, causing quiet to descend on those they passed.

Private Mijares stopped before a tent larger than the others.

"Stay here," he told the boys.

Dismounting, he limped over and saluted a guard standing just inside the tent's shadow.

"What's he saying?" asked Trino.

"I guess he's telling them who we are."

"If the guards let us pass, the general should accept us, right?"

José shrugged. "Let's hope so. If not, we'll have a long ride back to Sahuayo, or maybe—"

Private Mijares came hobbling back from the entrance to the tent. Climbing up on his horse, he motioned to the boys. "General Mendoza will talk to you tomorrow morning," he stated matter-of-factly. "We'll get something to eat now."

José opened his mouth to speak, but Mijares was already guiding them down a small incline. At its foot, they pulled up before a long wooden post at which other horses stood tied.

"The kitchen's on the other side of that fire," he said, pointing. "We'll tie up the animals here."

"What about food for them?" asked José.

"Let's look for food for us and them."

The three set off into camp. Scores of tents stretched

away in all directions. As they walked, José noticed that most of the tents formed circles, and in the open spaces sat the campfires.

Many of the men were slowly making their way back to their tents, and some hailed them with a hello, or a good night, before continuing on their way.

Private Mijares escorted them to a largish tent with no sides. Piles of crates formed its chest-high walls. As they walked up to the entrance, voices came from within.

"I'm telling you, we need more meat," said a deep voice.

"Look, I'm just the go-between. I give you what the women give me," said another voice.

"Well then, we'll have to send these soldiers out to hunt for deer and rabbits. The Lord knows they can't live off vegetables much longer."

Private Mijares limped up to the tent, and the boys followed.

A slim-looking soldier stood in the middle of the opening. At his side on an upside-down pot sat a short plump man in white. "Well, what do we have here?" he asked, hopping to his feet.

"Some hungry mouths to feed, if you have any left-overs," answered Private Mijares.

"Why of course," replied the man in white with a sweeping bow. "Let me introduce myself first. I am Chef Gustavo. Welcome to my kitchen."

"I'm José Sánchez del Río, from Sahuayo."

"I'm José Trinidad Flores Espinosa, and I'm from Sahuayo too."

"Sahuayo, eh?" said the cook, turning and heading back among an assortment of kettles and boxes. "You don't happen to have any extra chickens there, do you? If you ask me, this vegetable stew could certainly use some."

José chuckled. "No, we're low on chickens too," he said.

As the boys sat themselves down on the boxes, the cook held up a pot and asked, "When was the last time you ate? You haven't come all the way here on empty stomachs, have you?"

"Not quite," answered José. "This morning, in Quitupan, Señora Chávez fixed us some terrific chilaquiles."

The clatter of pots and pans went silent.

"You said *what*?" asked the chef, a look of alarm spreading across his face.

"Chilaquiles," said José, looking from one man to the other. "They were really tasty." Still confused, he added, "What do you have against chilaquiles?"

The thin soldier spoke up now for the first time since their arrival. "You must forgive my dear friend, the chef," he said, addressing José. "It's not the chilaquiles he finds fault with; it's the Chávez family."

"Why?" asked Trino. "What's wrong with them?"

"Señor Chávez," answered the soldier, "is a federal agent."

"And you mean to tell me they fed you, stabled your horse, gave you a place to sleep, and sent you on your way, knowing all the while you were on your way to *us*?" General Mendoza asked the boys the next morning.

"Yes, General, sir, that's what I said. I told Señor Chávez that we wanted to find the Cristeros. He was so kind, and his wife made such—"

"I don't want to hear about her cooking, my young —what's your name again?"

"José—José Sánchez del Río."

"Yes, José. What amazes me is that they didn't tie up you and your friend right there and send you to México City. I just don't understand."

Ever since he entered, José had been stealing glances about the large tent. In the center stood a small desk covered with maps and papers. Behind it sat two men, who introduced themselves as General Prudencio Mendoza and General Luis Morfín. Piles of ammunition lined the side walls. In the back, long red sticks stacked one atop another formed a three-foot wall. *Dynamite*, thought José.

All through General Mendoza's interrogation, General Morfín sat to the side, fiddling with a pair of binoculars which dangled from his neck. Now he spoke. "Perhaps Señor Chávez didn't think two boys could do much to help our cause," he hazarded.

"Good point, Morfín," said General Mendoza. Shifting his large frame once again toward José and Trino, he fixed them with a stare. Holding them in his gaze, he drew a monocle from the front pocket of his shirt and placed it on his left eye.

"And why, might I ask, did you two come all this way?"

José took a deep breath and stared the general back in the eyes. "We want to be Cristeros and fight for Christ the King."

"And at your age, how do you exactly," he paused, fingering his monocle, "propose to do that?"

"I know I'm too young to use a rifle, but I can help in other ways. I know how to take care of horses, I can oil rifles, I can cook—"

General Mendoza's gaze had begun to wander off in the distance. General Morfín seemed to be cleaning his binoculars. A thought jumped into José's head. *Oh yeah, why didn't I tell them before?*

"—and I can play trumpet," he finished.

At this, General Morfín let his binoculars fall.

"Mendoza," he said, "that reminds me. You heard about Jorge, didn't you?"

"You mean your bugler?"

"Right. He could use a helper. None of the other men can squeeze a noise out of that blasted horn. And come to think of it, the flag bearer—"

"I see, I see, Morfín. If you need the boy, you can take him, just do me one favor—keep him away from the fighting."

"That can be arranged," he said, turning around. "The name's Morfín, General Morfín, and you?"

"I'm José Sánchez del Río," said the boy, breathing a sigh of relief.

"Well, José, you'll be coming with me," said the general. "What about the other one?" he asked, turning to face General Mendoza, who was now twirling the monocle between his fingers.

The general sat up and slipped the eyepiece back between his cheek and eyebrow, fixing Trino with a stare.

"You said your name was—"

"Trino, short for José Trinidad Flores Espinosa."

"Very well, Trino," continued the general. "What do you have to say for yourself?"

Trino raised his head. "I want to fight with the Cristeros too. I'll do anything you need me to. I'm ready to help."

"And he's a pretty good shot," added José.

Trino smiled.

"Hmm," said General Mendoza. "What do you say, Morfín?"

"Those federales already had their opportunity to capture you two," he said, looking from boy to boy. "Unless you go seeking it, I doubt they'll get another chance."

José and Trino left with General Morfín, and as they wound their way through the clusters of tents, group after group of soldiers stood and saluted. José noticed that many of their eyes weren't turned toward the general, but to him and Trino.

"My army is stationed over there," said General Morfín, pointing ahead to one of the large circles of tents.

"Do you always travel with General Mendoza?" asked José.

"Not always," answered Morfín. "In fact, we arrived yesterday, and I'm planning on moving north next week. We try to stay on the move to keep the federals guessing."

"What about Chef Gustavo? Does he travel with you?" questioned Trino.

"No, though I wish he did. Chef Gustavo is General Mendoza's cook. We make do without him, though it is nice to have a decent meal now and then."

They stopped outside a little brown tent.

"Let me think," said the general. "We need to find you a place to stay. José, you'll be close to my tent. Trino, I'll put you with Lieutenant Gódinez."

"Yes, sir," said Trino. "Do I get a rifle?"

"We'll see, we'll see."

"Um, General Morfín?" asked José, sheepishly.

"Yes, son?"

"I was thinking that if the federals find out I've joined the Cristeros, they might try to punish my family."

"Well, yes, that's possible," answered the general, eyeing José. "It's part of the risk."

"Do you think . . . well, could I have a battle name —you know, one that wouldn't reveal my identity?"

"Hmmm. Not so bad an idea," said the general, sliding his hand up and down the strap of his binoculars. "A name that's different enough to confuse them, but not so different that it confuses us."

"How about Cuauhtémoc?" said Trino with a giggle.

"No," said General Morfín. "Let's keep it simple. José, from now on, your battle name will be *José Luis.*"

~

"Gosh, Trino, I can't feel my hand anymore. We've been polishing boots for hours. How am I supposed to ride a horse now?"

"And how am I supposed to fire a gun? My hand feels like a *burro* stepped on it."

"Looks like you've been polishing *it* instead of boots."

Trino wearily dropped his rag and said, "Why polish them? I think the scuffs and scratches make them look tougher."

"Next time Private Mijares sticks his head in here, let's interrogate him."

"Better yet," said Trino, "let's hypnotize him and make *him* do the polishing."

"Yeah, good idea. You hypnotize him, and I'll supply him with boots."

Trino looked up from his work. "Someone's coming," he said.

The canvas tent flap moved, and light poured inside. In stepped Private Mijares.

"And how are my young Cristeros getting along?" he asked, surveying their work.

"Half-dead," said Trino.

"Not dead yet, but getting there," added José.

Mijares glanced at his watch. "I left you with this job three hours ago, and you already want to call it quits?"

"No," said José quickly. "I didn't say anything about quitting."

"Good, good," replied the private. "I've come to rescue you from polishing duty. Clean up here and meet me in the munitions tent."

"Yes, sir," said José, jumping to his feet.

"Guess we don't have to hypnotize anybody after all," said Trino.

When the boys arrived at the munitions tent, the private showed them guns that needed cleaning. After a brief explanation of what to do, he left.

"You spoke too soon about our not needing to hypnotize anyone, Trino," said José.

"Well, at least guns are more exciting than boots."

A couple hours later, both boys were only very slowly rubbing the rusty guns with oil.

Guns are more exciting than boots, Trino told himself. *Guns are more exciting than b . . ."* He jerked himself awake with a start. "I can't do this anymore," he said, setting down the rusty old rifle.

"Don't do that," said José sleepily as he squirted a drop of oil onto a knob and then started working it back and forth with his finger.

"So much cleaning—and no firing," Trino said with a yawn. "I want to see these things work."

"I just want to see if I can hit anything," said José.

"That's not hard. You just wait till you're calm, take aim, breathe out, and squeeze."

"Calm," said José, rubbing a rag up and down the long barrel of a Mauser. "That's the problem. How can you be calm in the middle of a battle?"

"I don't know," replied Trino, turning back to his work. "Guess I'll have to wait till the real thing to find out."

～

Later that night, flames leaped high into the air from a mammoth pile of wood. Rings of soldiers sat, cross-legged, all about.

Grasping his rosary between weary fingers, José got to his feet. "The third joyful mystery," he announced, "is the birth of Baby Jesus in Bethlehem."

As he finished the first half of the Hail Mary, his eyes swept around the circle.

It feels so different, he thought, as he waited for the soldiers to finish their part. *I'm praying about the first*

Christmas with Mary and Joseph and Baby Jesus, and here I am so far from home—like them.

"Hail Mary, full of grace, the Lord is with thee . . ." he continued. "And blessed is the fruit of thy womb, Jesus."

After the Rosary, the soldiers broke into groups and slowly made their way back to where they slept, some in tents, others in the open.

As José gazed up at the stars from beneath his blanket, it dawned on him: *I may be far from home, but this is where I belong, just as Baby Jesus belonged in Bethlehem that first Christmas night. I'm sure he's happy to see me here, fighting for him.*

He pulled the blanket over his head and sleep overtook him.

9

THE BUGLER

H UH . . . ? Go away."
"Get up, sleepy-head. It's time to wake the army."
José pulled the blanket away from his head and slowly pried an eyelid open. The sky was still black and ablaze with stars.

"Come on, son," said the soldier who had awoken José. "You've got to play that little horn of yours for us."

"One second. . . . Let me get my shoes on."

As he slipped on his boots, thoughts came flickering through his head. The last three weeks with the Cristeros seemed like a blur of more odd jobs than he could remember. He had scrubbed pots and dishes, cleaned and oiled countless rifles, helped Chef Gustavo cook beans and tortillas, taken care of horses, carried water back and forth, minded the big campfire, helped soldiers take off their spurs, cleaned boots, served coffee, and run all kinds of errands.

After ten days, General Morfín called José to his tent for the first time since they met. "Two things," the general told him. "First, I want you to be my bugler. That means you have to learn the calls. Second, I want you to be my flag bearer. Whenever we're on the move, you don't leave my side."

José had spent the rest of the day nearly jumping from place to place he was so excited.

"The problem with being bugler during war," explained Jorge, the head bugler, "is that you can't practice. Any noise you make, the men assume it's a command. So every chance you get to play for real you have to use as practice—there's no better way to learn bugle."

After he had crawled out of bed and slipped on his shoes, José began to blast the shrill notes on his little horn. Grunts and yawns poured from the sleeping forms on the ground and from inside the tents. Some soldiers didn't stir until their companions gave them a jab in the side. Others jumped up quickly and tidied themselves and their sleeping areas.

After ten minutes, all of the men had assembled in front of General Morfín's tent. Morfín stepped out, binoculars dangling from his neck.

"Kneel down, soldiers of Christ the King," he said.

Everyone, oldest to youngest—even the general himself—knelt on the dusty ground to offer their day to God.

Later that morning, a new boy strode into camp. He came across José and Trino as they hovered around a large wooden box.

"What are you doing?" asked the boy.

Trino paused in the middle of folding a piece of white cloth. José held a large red book in his hand.

"Straightening up after Mass," answered Trino, looking up at the newcomer. The boy was short and had dark skin and the flat face of an Indian.

"What's your name?" Trino asked.

"I'm Lorenzo," he answered.

"Welcome to the Cristeros," said José, smiling. "I'm José Luis, and this is Trino." The boys shook hands.

"Do you always have Mass?" asked Lorenzo, peering into the open box.

"No," answered José. "Just when there's a priest here."

"Who said Mass today?"

"Padre Tomás," answered Trino, "but he just left for another camp."

"Does he say Mass out here in the open?"

"Sí," Trino replied. "We built a small portable altar, and the soldiers assemble there with their rifles and flags and all. José and I get to serve. It's great, especially when Padre gives Communion to all the men."

"As a Cristero," added José, "every time you receive Communion, you know it could be your last."

∼

That afternoon, José reported for duty. General Morfín was studying some papers strewn across his desk.

"Where's your horse?" asked the general as José walked in.

"Oh, Copper? He's tied up with the others."

"Well, José—*José Luis*—you'd better go saddle him up. We ride in ten minutes."

José hurried down the path toward the horses, flag in hand. Most of the other men had already left. A few stragglers were adjusting their saddles and cantering off.

Copper's ears gave a twitch as José called his name. The boy leaned the flag against a fence and struggled to lift his saddle into place. His trembling fingers didn't seem to remember how to fasten the buckles. He paused with bridle in hand.

"We can do this, right, boy? This is what we came here for." He leaned his head against the horse's neck. Copper whinnied and stamped a foot.

After cinching the saddle and slipping the bit between the animal's teeth, José buckled the bridle straps and climbed onto the horse. Grabbing the flag, he gave a flick on the reins, and Copper started off.

General Morfín was waiting by his tent. He sat atop what looked like a mustang—white and brown with flecks of black.

"Ready?" he asked, setting off at a trot.

"Yes, sir!" replied José, following the general's lead.

"I want you to stay close by me and out of trouble," said Morfín as they trotted along. "The men look to the flag for assurance. If you go down, it spells disaster. Understand?"

José nodded.

"Do you remember your bugle calls?"

"Yes, sir, General, sir," José replied.

By now the two had reached a clearing where the other soldiers waited atop their horses.

The general rode through the center of his troops, and then paused to talk with his aides before trotting off.

The mass of men started forward ever so slowly behind their general. José glanced up at the flag in his hands. It was green, white, and red and bore the words "Viva Cristo Rey y Nuestra Señora de Guadalupe." Emblazoned in the center was Our Lady of Guadalupe.

As they drew near the forest, José kept his eyes on General Morfín. The general's mustang started to pick up speed.

Tucking the flag against his side, José lowered his head below the branches whipping past.

Copper was following close upon the heels of Morfín's horse. Both animals raced down the hillside. José peeked to his right and noticed another horse galloping alongside them.

These Cristeros are crazy, he thought.

After several minutes of plunging down the hill and through the forest, an open patch came into view ahead. Soon they were speeding across a field of grass and small bushes.

José unfurled the flag. Wind tore at it, dragging the pole backward.

"You take care of directions, Copper," he hollered, "and I'll take care of the flag." The horse seemed to like this plan, for with an extra burst of speed he pulled even with General Morfín's mustang.

Now they were riding down the side of a valley between two mountain ranges. The scrub brush gave way to flat ground. To his left, José saw a small cluster of houses sitting on the grassy plain. Farther ahead lay another, bigger group.

Once past the houses, General Morfín slowed to a trot. As the other riders started to bunch up behind, he pulled his horse to a halt. Binoculars to his eyes, he gazed back and forth along the horizon.

José looked in the same direction, but all he could see were the bushes near at hand, and the hills far away.

Before long, the other Cristeros arrived on the scene. Soon they formed a huge semicircle with General Morfín in the center. By his side, José sat atop Copper, flag unfurled.

"Men," spoke General Morfín after the last horse had pulled to a stop, "our scouts tell me that a group of federal soldiers from Quitupan are on patrol south of Cotija.

"Yesterday they started a slow movement in our direction, and they should be nearing the hills in the middle of the valley soon. Now I know it will be dark soon, but we'll have the element of surprise. If we get there before them and manage to take the high ground, I believe we can inflict heavy casualties. It might make them rethink their offensive entirely. My hope is that we can do this without losing any of our men.

"I want to be sure you men know why we fight."

All eyes were fixed on him now.

"We aren't vigilantes out to cause trouble. Nor are we fighting for just a man, or even for a group of men. This army is different." The general let his gaze drift from face to face.

"I know why I'm here—to fight the unjust oppression of our present government and to restore freedom of worship to our people. I'd rather achieve this without war, but war is our only choice.

"You who fight with me," continued Morfín, extending his hand, "I hope you understand this. Never forget why we fight. Whatever happens today, or any other day, we will not stop until they give us back our churches . . . or we all die fighting."

Morfín swallowed. "Any man who doesn't want this is free to leave right now. We'll ask no questions, and hold no grudges."

The soldiers shuffled in their saddles and looked around at their companions. José gripped the flag, his heart beating wildly. The general waited a moment in silence, then nodded.

"Stay by my side, boy," he whispered to José.

Raising his rifle high in the air, he shouted, "Vamos. Viva Cristo Rey!"

"Viva Cristo Rey, y Viva la Vírgen de Guadalupe!" the men shouted back, raising their rifles high.

A smile shone across José's face. This was just how he had imagined life in the Cristeros would be. He thought back to last week, when General Morfín had given him his own rifle.

"Yours to have—not to use, unless there's grave need," the general had told him.

After descending the mountain, the army moved slowly. General Morfín made his way through shaded valleys and hollows, attempting to mask his troops' movements from unfriendly eyes.

He was astute, this short man with binoculars. He planned all his attacks meticulously, for never once did he hesitate, or pause to study a map. Half an hour after they had left their rallying point, he had his troops lined up at the foot of a small grassy hill. All was quiet.

The hill rose above them about two hundred feet. Its sides were mainly open, with a few trees and bushes scattered about.

Movement in some tall grass at the base of the hill caught José's attention.

"*Qué hay*, Pato?" asked General Morfín.

The grass stopped moving, and a man pulled himself up from the ground. He ambled over to the general and saluted.

"Not twenty minutes ago they were about three miles off, headed straight this way, *mi general.* They should be in position soon."

"I wish I could see through this hill right now," muttered the general. "What about their numbers?"

"Well, sir," replied the scout, "I didn't have the best observation post. But there is at least a battalion."

General Morfín played with his binoculars.

"With all due respect, sir, I think that now is the moment," continued the scout. "They wouldn't expect us to attack them out here in the open, and especially this late in the day."

"I see what you mean," replied Morfín. His eyebrows were gathered into furrows, and his eyes shut for a moment.

No one moved.

Then the general spoke.

"The sun's almost down—so we have little time. There will be three movements. The first time you hear the bugle, that's for Camacho on the left. You'll show yourselves but then take up defensive positions. The second blast is for Attila in the front. You'll charge down the hill. Villa, the third blast is for you and your men. You'll circle los federales and take them from behind."

The men nodded.

"Villa, you first," said the general, motioning.

A group of soldiers started off to the right.

"Camacho, you're next."

Another group of men set off around the left side of the hill.

"Your turn, Attila, and stay low up top. Wait for my signal."

This last group of soldiers started up the center of the hill. General Morfín followed them, a little back and to the left.

José took the rear. Sweat began to line his palms as he gripped the flag.

The hill was an easy climb for the horses. Just below the summit, General Morfín dismounted and gave his reins to José. Then he slowly walked the little distance that remained to the top.

José glanced to his right and saw the soldiers loading their rifles. His eyes strayed down to his own weapon. It was a bit rusty in places, and the barrel had a few long scratches. *Hope I don't have to use this thing*, he thought.

Seconds later, a low whistle caught his attention. General Morfín was waving from just below the top of the hill. The general held his hand up, palm toward José. Then he began a countdown with his fingers.

The bugle—where was it? Hanging from his neck. But he only had two hands. Hoping the general's horse would stay put, José released the reins and scrambled for his instrument. As he lifted the mouthpiece to his lips, he racked his brain to remember the notes for "Charge".

The general dropped the last of his fingers just as José realized in horror that he had forgotten the call.

To make matters worse, the mustang at his side, now conscious of its freedom, started up the hill. Morfín waved his arms in frustration.

At last he remembered and blew one long, drawn-out blast.

"Better than nothing," said José, letting the instrument fall from his lips.

To José's joy, the stray mustang had made straight for General Morfín. The boy dismounted and walked Copper up the rest of the hill. On reaching the summit, he let out a sigh. The troops had understood. Cristero soldiers were streaming out from the left.

Down on the plain, a serpentine mass of gray was weaving its way toward them between the small hills.

"Sorry about the bugle," said José.

"Forget about it," answered Morfín, still glued to his binoculars. "I'm worried about los federales—there's more than I thought. You remember the notes for 'Retreat' don't you?"

"Sí, mi general."

"Good. We might need it. But first, I'm going to send Attila and his men down there. You be ready with your bugle."

As José and General Morfín watched in the fading light, the two Cristero columns made their way through the brush and over the small hills that separated them from the federals in gray.

Camacho's soldiers on the left began taking positions behind boulders and bushes. On the right, Villa and his men made for the rear of the federal troops. Camacho was the bait; Villa the trap.

"Now. Signal another charge."

Remembering the notes this time, José put the bugle to his lips and blew with all his might. Springing up from where they had been hiding to his left, Attila's men came pouring over the top of the hill and into view of the approaching federals.

"Good, that scared them," said General Morfín, surveying the action below. "We might do some damage yet."

The body of federal troops had now halted in the narrow valley. To the left, Camacho's soldiers began to rush out against the federal flank. With Attila and his men pouring down the hill front, the federals started to pull back.

"Look at the fools," said General Morfín, gazing through his binoculars. "They're spread out as thin as a teaspoon of tequila on a frying pan."

As José watched from beside Copper, the federal troops continued to pull back. "They're retreating, aren't they?" he asked.

General Morfín seemed not to hear. Through his binoculars he scanned the horizon apprehensively. "It will be dark soon," he murmured. "We'd better finish this up soon. José, blow that horn of yours again. It's time for Villa to take them from behind."

José raised the gleaming instrument to his lips and blasted out the correct notes once again.

Far out upon the plain, a dark blur streamed out from the right.

"They're supposed to hit from behind, not from the side!" fumed Morfín. "What's gotten into their heads this time?"

The Cristero soldiers under Villa had collided with the federal troops about two-thirds of the way down their main column. From where Jose and the general stood, all they could hear were the shouts of the men and bullets firing.

"Looks like this could turn into a bloodbath," said Morfín despondently. "Call them off."

José turned to the general and hesitated.

"Come on, boy, you heard what I said. Take that blasted horn of yours and sound retreat!"

José remembered the notes and obeyed.

"Well now," said the general, surveying the scene below. "Let's see if our men can make it back safely in the darkness."

~

"You should have seen their faces when we poured out from behind that hill."

"Sí, their general was right there, next to his horse, and he took off running. Salcido got the horse *and* the general's sword."

"Was it that white horse you brought back?"

"That's the one, a real beauty."

The bonfire burned bright and tall amid the circle of seated men. The Cristeros had made it back to their camp safely, and once there, the day's battle had been all they talked about.

"We gave the captured horse to General Morfín. He called it '*un caballo noble*'," said one of the men to his companion.

"We'll need to do more than just steal horses and swords if we want to win this war," said a third man.

"We didn't take any hostages, and there weren't any casualties either."

"That was because it was already dark," said the first man. "Give us some daylight, and we'll finish that army off."

~

"And blessed is the fruit of thy womb, Jesus." José led the men in a Rosary of thanksgiving for the successful operation.

On the opposite side of the circle, a grizzled soldier sat with his legs crossed, cigarette dangling from his lip. "Look at him," he said, giving his friend a kick.

"What?" replied the man, stirring from his nap.

"Reminds me of Saint Tarsicius, he does, leading us all like that."

"You mean little José Luis?"

"Fourteen, and he's already a Cristero."

"I sure hope he lasts. In my book, boys his age only

make easy targets for federal bullets," said the second man matter-of-factly.

"That," said the old soldier, slowly snuffing out his cigarette, "is why he reminds me of Tarsicius."

10

PICAZO'S PLAN

TWO DAYS LATER, row upon row of rifles gleamed in the morning sunlight. Padre Tomás had arrived the night before and was celebrating Mass for the troops at a portable altar.

"*Dominus vobiscum*," said the priest in a low voice.

"*Et cum spiritu tuo*," replied José, hands folded.

A whinny came from behind the clump of trees.

"Isn't that General Morfín's new horse?" asked José, whispering.

"Sí," replied Trino, who stood by his side, "*pero qué pasa?*"

The animal started pulling at its rope. Now the other horses started to stir as well.

Meanwhile, the men seemed not to notice. Most of them knelt on the ground, praying.

José's eye caught movement off in the distance. *What is that?* he thought, gazing out over the heads of the Cristeros. He saw metal glinting in the sun.

"Someone's coming!" he shouted.

Instantly, a hundred heads turned and stared in José's direction. For a moment, he felt like a fool; then he pointed a trembling hand toward the north.

"Los federales!" shouted a voice. The phrase was taken up and repeated, "Los federales, los federales!"

Some of the troops jumped to their feet. Others dropped to their bellies.

Some of the men had already lain down in the grass to take up positions. They trained their rifles in the direction of the attackers.

"We don't have bullets!" said a voice. "We can't fight like this!"

"*Cállate!*" cried another voice. It was the general, binoculars in hand.

"Men, this valley is no place to fight," he shouted. "I want you to separate, find ammunition, and regroup on the ridge." He pointed to the line of peaks behind him. The men held their silence.

"Now! Let's move it!" shouted the general.

As the men headed off, José tugged on the white vestment Father Tomás was wearing. "Padre, what do we do about the things for Mass?"

"We'll take the important things with us. Here, you help with the ciborium, and Trino, you take the Missal —and we'll leave the altar."

"Padre, let's go," shouted a Cristero soldier.

The small group was well hidden in the forest by the time federal soldiers came into sight.

~

"It could have been a lot worse," said Padre Tomás when he and the boys returned to the spot where they had tried to have Mass that morning.

"Sí," added Trino, "If it weren't for José Luis, we could have all been captured."

"It wasn't me," protested José, walking along beside the other two. "The general's horse gave the alarm."

"You *and* the general's horse," corrected Padre Tomás.

The federal troops did not press their luck when they found the Cristeros gone. After grabbing everything of value, they headed off again. The two boys and the priest had returned to see what had been left behind.

"What about the portable altar?" asked José. "Why would they want that?"

"*No sé*," replied the padre. "We'll have to find something to take its place. I'm just glad that's the biggest thing they captured."

~

In his corner office, Rafael Picazo listened to the federal general explain the day's events. Though not an army officer, Picazo oversaw the federal government's efforts against the Cristeros in his region.

"We reached their camp, but somehow they knew beforehand that we were coming," the general said.

"You're not impressing me, General Tranquilino. We can't win this war through evading real battles."

"That's true, sir, but if we keep hoping that they'll come and fight us in the open, this war will last another hundred years."

"Look, General, I really don't care exactly what you do. The way I see it, we have to take out their leadership. Cut off the head," here he sliced his hand across his neck, "and the body shrivels up."

"Sir, let me get this straight: You're asking me to change the whole objective of this mission?"

The mayor pulled the cigar from between his teeth, leaned forward, and whispered, "What do you think the president will say when he receives the telegram announcing that you've captured a Cristero general?"

Stepping back, General Tranquilino's right hand wandered up to the rows of medals and pins on his chest.

"How do you suppose I go about capturing a general?"

Picazo made his way over to the window that looked out on the town square. His reflection stared back at him. Adjusting his moustache, he said, "Only a general knows another general's games. Where are you at your most vulnerable? How could they capture you? Think up a plan—I'm sure you'll do fine."

General Tranquilino nodded his head. "I'll figure something out; I'm sure. We ride in half an hour."

"Good. I'll be waiting for news of the capture. There's plenty of space in my jail."

~

José gazed at the scenery as he rode along. Flowers were blooming in all the trees they passed. *Spring is already here*, he thought. *I can't wait until we can have fresh mangos again.*

He pulled his horse level with the general's mustang. "Any orders, sir?" he asked.

"Nothing special today," said General Morfín, sauntering along. "Just a few telephone lines to cut south of Cotija."

"Yes, sir," replied José.

After the surprise attack during Mass, the Cristeros had changed camp and hidden in the forest for several days. One of the women who brought them food had given José a letter from his parents. In it, they told him of their plans to move to Guadalajara for the rest of the war. Things were becoming too dangerous in Sahuayo.

"General Morfín?"

"Yes, José Luis?"

"How did the federal soldiers know where our camp was?"

The general shook his head. "No idea," he said.

"What if they're still following us?" asked the boy.

"Then God save us."

~

"Are you sure the Cristero scum will pass by here?" demanded the soldier. His gray uniform matched the column of men stretching behind him into the woods. They stood in the shade of the trees lining a long, narrow valley. The valley itself was open grassland, and the trees provided excellent cover.

"Sí, Señor," replied the peasant, "this is the only way."

"If you're wrong, you'll regret it," growled the soldier, pushing the man away. He turned to the group of men.

"Spread out along the tree line here, and take cover," he said. "We attack when I give the word. Remember," he stated emphatically, waving his index finger, "we want General Morfín alive."

"How much farther?" demanded General Morfín.

"This hut is about halfway down the valley," said the scout, pointing to a little brick structure on their left. "We'll reach the plains in five minutes. The telephone lines are right there."

"Should be easy, right?" asked the general, from his white horse.

"If your men are ready," replied the scout.

José rode along on Copper. *Seems simple enough*, he thought to himself. *But I still can't wait till we're done with this job.*

Just then, a loud crack came from the woods. General Morfín's horse reared up and then fell backward.

"It's an ambush!" shouted the scout, turning his horse and galloping off.

∽

"Good shot."

"What about the other horse, the one with the boy?"

"Let it go, the boy will bolt. We want the old man."

"What if they both ride off?"

"They won't get far on one horse."

"Men, keep your weapons out. Morfín's too smart to fight all of us, but he might try something fast. Whatever happens, we take him alive. Let's move."

"My horse—where . . . how?" gasped the general.

Blood poured from his horse's side, and the animal struggled weakly.

"Up by the trees, look," said José, who had pulled to a halt beside where the general lay sprawled in the grass.

Morfín scrambled to his feet and stared. Below them on the plain the Cristero line was already fragmented. "José, flee, now," he said, still trying to catch his breath from the fall.

"Mi general, no!"

"It's a trap. Go—now! I'll be all right."

José watched the figures in gray pouring out of the trees from behind the hut. The Cristero soldiers were fleeing in all directions. He turned to General Morfín and shook his head. "Mi general," said the boy, jumping off Copper and holding out the reins, "you take my horse."

Morfín shook his head and pointed. "*Muchacho!* Are you mad? Fly, now!"

"Look, General, take my horse and save yourself. You're more necessary for the cause than me. I'll be all right."

General Morfín glanced at the advancing troops again. The federal soldiers were only seconds away.

"God be with you, son," said Morfín, gently laying a hand on José's shoulder.

Putting a foot in the stirrup, the general quickly

swung himself up onto Copper. José barely touched the horse's side just as Morfín flicked the reins.

A lone figure stood in the valley.

 ⌒

"There goes the boy," announced one of the soldiers as they galloped along.

"Good. Just one old man left now."

"Hey, who gets the reward for all this?"

"Mind your own business. You'll get paid."

"But—"

Bang! A loud explosion came from the valley's bottom, and a bullet hissed past their heads.

"Everyone find cover, now!"

The federal soldiers spurred their horses to the small brick farmhouse on their right.

Once in its shadow, they dismounted.

"You should have let me shoot him."

"Quiet! He isn't worth anything dead."

"Neither are we!"

"You don't look dead yet. Listen to me. You four spread out and come from behind. I'll take the center. All we have to do is grab him."

"Just give me one shot, and he's ours."

"No way. You heard me. We're taking him alive."

 ⌒

In the hollow of the valley, José's fingers trembled as he tried to pull back the bolt on his rifle. The dead horse felt warm against his side. In his hand, the bullet didn't want to fit into the hot firing chamber. When at last the chamber opened, the cartridge slipped from his hand and fell to the ground.

"Why didn't I practice more?" he asked himself, managing to slide another bullet into place.

Turning, he peeked over the horse's belly. "What?" he exclaimed.

Only one figure remained where before there had been five.

He scanned to the left and right—nothing—just one man approaching slowly. A heavy silence filled the valley. Leaning his weapon across the horse's belly, José trained it on the lone figure in gray. The sweaty palm of his index finger touched the cold metal trigger. He squeezed.

Suddenly, José heard shouts from behind his back. Before he could move, powerful hands grabbed him and crushed him to the ground.

"Got him!" said a voice.

José was a prisoner.

II

THE PRISONERS

THE DOOR SWUNG OPEN, and blinding sunlight sliced through the darkness. A vague outline material- ized in the doorway. Someone gasped, and then there came a thump. All was still.

Except the crying.

"Qué pasa?"

"Who's that?" said a high voice, inhaling quickly.

"Wait a minute, you sound familiar. Is that you, Lorenzo?"

"José?" asked the high voice.

"*Híjole!* Lorenzo, am I glad to see you."

José walked over to his little friend and helped him to his feet. "How did you end up here?" he asked, grabbing the boy by the shoulders.

"I was in the rear guard. We saw the federals attack. Next thing I knew we were surrounded. I don't know what happened to the others."

As he finished his story, both boys sat down and leaned back against the wall.

"What about you, José—what happened to you?"

"Well, I was with General Morfín, and we were going to cut some telephone lines. Then his horse got shot. It was a trap. So I gave him my horse. Then I covered his escape. I was just about to shoot one of the federals, when a big fellow jumped on me from behind and pinned me to the ground. When they realized that I wasn't the general, they went crazy. They kicked me and hit me and tossed me around. Four of them aimed their rifles right at me, and I thought I was *muerto*. But a fifth one screamed at them to stop. I think he was an officer. He offered me my freedom if I would join his side. I told him that they had captured me because my ammo ran out and that I wasn't going to give up just like that. Then they tied my hands and put a rope around my neck, and threw me in this hut."

"What will they do with us?" asked Lorenzo.

"No idea," replied José. "Maybe just send us home. I'm from Sahuayo. What about you?"

"Me?—I'm from Jiquilpan."

"That's close to Sahuayo. I had to pass by it on my way to join the Cristeros."

"Well, I've never been to Sahuayo. I sure hope they send me back home."

"I hope so too, Lorenzo."

~

In his office, Rafael Picazo crumpled the paper in the palm of his hand and squeezed. Then, snatching the cigar from his mouth, he screamed in frustration, "*Tontos!* They can't even catch a miserable Cristero general!" He threw the wad on the floor and added, "What good is some boy to me?"

In the corner, by the door, the messenger in gray trembled. "I wasn't in the battle, sir—"

"I didn't ask your opinion," broke in Picazo, fingering his moustache. "Give me some paper."

Dipping his pen in the inkstand, Picazo hesitated. "Do I want this boy?" he wondered aloud.

The messenger didn't move.

"I asked you a question," said Picazo, clenching his teeth.

"Sí, Señor. No, Señor. Ahh . . . *No sé.*"

Picazo was now nodding his head. "So that's what you think, is it?"

"Sí, Señor."

"Good thing you're just delivering messages."

Popping his cigar back into place, Picazo took the pen and held it over the paper.

> Tranquilino—
>
> Disappointed.
> Think up new plan.
> Send boy to me.
> Both boys.
> I'll take care of them.
>
> —Picazo

⁓

Meanwhile in the hut, José strained his eyes in the dim light to write a message of his own. The federal guard had given him pen and paper.

Cotija Monday, February 6 of 1928

My dear Mamá,

I was taken prisoner in battle today. I think that soon I will die, but that doesn't matter, Mamá. Please accept the will of God—I die very happy, because I die in battle alongside our Lord.

Don't you worry about me dying; your worrying is what would be hardest for me. Tell my brothers to follow their littlest brother's example, and you do the will of God. Take courage, and send me your blessing along with Papá's.

Say good-bye to everyone for me one last time, and finally, may you receive the heart of your son who loves you so dearly and wants to see you so much before he dies.

José Sánchez del Río

"Better prepare her for the worst, right, Lorenzo?" said José, folding up the letter.

Lorenzo shifted as he sat. "José, does it hurt to die?"

José gulped. "I don't know. I hope it's quick."

Lorenzo nervously rubbed his knee. "José, are we going to die?"

Setting down his pen and paper and slowly exhaling, José shut his eyes. Leaning forward, he cradled his head between his two hands.

"*No sé*, Lorenzo. I really don't know."

Outside the little hut, two men debated.

"One horse."

"You sure?"

"Just do what I say, private. If they refuse my offer, we're sending them straight to Picazo."

"Yes, sir, General Tranquilino."

"Good. And tie their hands nice and stiff. Wouldn't want the only captives we have to escape, now would we?"

The two men stopped in front of the knotty wooden door.

"*Ábrela!*" said the general.

Private Gómez inserted a key and undid the padlock

hanging from a bar across the door. Setting this aside, he gave a tug and heaved it open.

"*Buenos días, prisioneros.* How are we doing this morning?"

The two boys were sprawled out next to each other asleep on the floor. Each of them—first one, then the other—lifted his head and looked around.

"Yes, you are prisoners, if you remember," said General Tranquilino.

"And who are you?" asked José, shielding his eyes from the glare.

"If you knew anything about an army," said the general, "you'd be able to tell from my medals."

He looked his captives up and down.

"Gómez," he whispered, "you sure these are the right ones?"

"What do you mean, sir?" asked the private, puzzled.

"They don't look like soldiers to me," replied the general.

Private Gómez made as if to speak, but General Tranquilino held up a hand.

"You boys don't know what you've gotten yourselves into. Bad things are in store for you. We . . . get rid of all the Cristeros we capture."

He paused to see the boys' reactions.

José scratched his short black hair. Lorenzo rubbed his eyes.

The general continued. "But me—I'm a nice fellow. I've decided to forgive you."

The boys perked up, really listening now.

"All you have to do . . ." he paused.

José and Lorenzo had now risen to their feet. "Is what?" José asked hopefully.

"All you have to do," he continued, "is join our side."

Both José and Lorenzo frowned.

"Look, boys, you've been fighting for the wrong side. The Cristero army is illegitimate, unofficial, and destined for failure. We federals stand for law and order. We stand for peace. You have fought against the legitimate government of your country and deserve to die. But I'll forgive you right here and now—let you go free—as long as you join our side."

The general folded his arms across his chest and looked from boy to boy.

José rubbed a hand through his disheveled hair. "Law and order?" he asked. "Was it law and order that murdered Anacleto Gonzàlez Flores? Was it law and order that came into our town and took over our churches? Was it law and order that wounded my uncle, Padre Ignacio?"

"You don't know what you're talking about, son; those are all complicated situations," replied the general.

"Freedom to go to church doesn't seem that complicated to me," José replied. "You want me to join your side?" he continued, clenching his fists. "Well, here's my answer: I'll never join the side of the persecutors of the Church. I'd rather die. I'm your enemy. Shoot me!"

~

"José, where are they taking us?" asked Lorenzo, his little frame jolting back and forth atop the horse. The boys had been traveling for several hours, blindfolded.

"Well," José replied, "we passed through Jiquilpan —that's where the lady gave us water and took the letter for my mother. So we must be heading north . . . I wonder how Copper's doing."

"Who's Copper—your dog?"

"My horse—the one that saved General Morfín's life."

"I'll bet he's better off than we are."

"Anything's better than having your hands tied, your eyes covered, and no idea where you're going."

"José, I don't get it," began Lorenzo.

"*Qué?*"

"You."

José was silent.

"What made you speak to the general like that? And what's going to happen to us now? He was furious with us, almost kicked that soldier. He took what you said as my answer too."

"What would you have said?" asked José, trying to

use his tongue to lift the bandana away from his eyes. It stayed in place.

"Something different—something that would not have gotten us into more trouble . . ."

"Lorenzo, I'm sorry," said José, as he heard his companion start to cry again.

"Lorenzo?" asked José after a while.

"Sí?" said the boy between sniffles.

"It's not as bad as it seems."

"Why's that?"

"Prisoners aren't allowed to talk," broke in a voice, menacingly.

"I won't talk if you take off this bandana," ventured José.

"General's orders," replied the voice.

"Where's the general now?"

"*Cállate, niño.* If you keep talking, you'll end up walking the rest of the way."

José and Lorenzo fell into an uneasy silence. From behind their blindfolds, all they could sense was which direction the sunlight was coming from. With their hands tied behind their backs, it was all they could do to hold on when their horse headed up or down hills.

Where are we going? José wondered.

~

The massive oak door lurched inward on its hinges. José held his breath.

"Welcome," said the soldier, pushing the two boys from behind. "Welcome to prison."

"No," whispered José, his voice dropping to a hush.

His face had lit up just moments earlier when the soldier had taken off their blindfolds. A quick glance around had revealed that they were standing in the atrium of his parish church, Santiago, in Sahuayo.

"This is *my* town," he had whispered to Lorenzo with pride.

Before his eyes could adjust to the darkness of the church, José had grown tense. The smell wafting up from the pews was not of incense, candles, or flowers. It was the smell of manure—fresh manure.

"Come on, this way," said the soldier giving a sharp tug on the rope. Lorenzo whimpered a little. The cord had been rubbing against his wrists all day, and now they were raw to the touch.

The soldier pulled them to the left. José wanted to tell him to watch out for the pews, but then he realized that there were no pews. Along the walls lay heaps of rubbish. A horse was nosing around in a pile of hay. At the foot of the altar smoldered a small fire. Odds and ends of what had been the pews lay scattered about. The statues in the niches behind the altar had been reduced to stumps of plaster. It looked as though someone had used them for target practice. Roosters wandered about, pecking at the ground.

The soldier led them along the back wall and into a small room with a vaulted roof. It was the baptistery.

In the center of the room stood the marble baptismal font. A grated window off to the side let in a few feeble rays of light.

The soldier untied them, saying, "Welcome to your new home."

~

Up in his corner office, Picazo listened to the messenger announce the boys' arrival.

"*Bueno*," he said, fumbling with his lighter. "I'll be down shortly."

"Sí, Señor," replied the soldier, turning on his heels and leaving the office.

"*Caray*," said Picazo to himself, as he gave the first puff on his cigar. "Don Macario can't seem to keep his brats out of trouble."

He sat down, and stared at the portrait of President Calles.

"Why did I ever have to become this kid's godfather?" he wondered aloud.

He looked again at the papers on his desk. The sentence for all rebel prisoners was death, and José had been caught red-handed. He shook his head.

"How can I please the president *and* save Macario's boy?"

~

After a whole day on horseback, neither boy had taken a seat in their new prison cell. Lorenzo was peering through the bars of the window into the street, while José examined the baptismal font.

A lone figure came striding through the church and into the baptistery. "On your feet, prisoners," barked the guard reflexively.

A frown spread across José's face.

Rafael Picazo stopped just feet away. "*Muchachos*," he said, spreading his palms, "what are two young men like you doing in a place like this?"

Silence. The two boys only stared.

Picazo gave a quick puff at his cigar and frowned. "José, what have you been up to?"

José looked at his godfather. "I've been off with the men, fighting," he said.

Picazo waved his smoking cigar in the air. "Fighting?" he asked. "That's not right. You should be in school, shouldn't you?" Without waiting for a response, he pulled a paper from his pocket. Lowering his voice, he took José by the shoulder and stepped aside.

"Look, son, these are my orders. You were captured fighting for the rebels. You know the sentence for that."

José nodded.

"Now listen. I know they tricked you into this. Your father and I have been good friends since we were boys.

I don't want to do what this paper says I have to do, for his sake," he paused, "and for yours."

He paused again to see what effect his words were having on the boy. José was listening.

Picazo dropped his voice to a hush. "Now, I've decided to put you on a train to Texas first thing tomorrow. You can wait out the war there. When things have calmed down here, we'll bring you back."

José stood in thought a little. He ran a hand through his hair. "Señor Picazo . . ."

"Yes, son, go on."

"I . . ."

Before he could continue, images and sounds arose in his mind: a campfire, surrounded by soldiers, blazing in the night; voices praying the Rosary; soldiers marching into battle; a horse with an empty saddle—his saddle; charging men without a flag bearer.

He hung his head, and then shook it. "No. No, I can't."

"Qué?" asked Picazo, tilting his head quizzically.

"Look, Señor Picazo, if you let me go, I'll join up with the Cristeros to fight again."

Picazo's face went red. The veins on his neck began to bulge. Before speaking, he inhaled deeply.

"I know what you mean, son. Once you've had a taste of battle, you thrive on it. If you want to become a soldier, so be it. I know some of the finest military schools around. I'm sure I can find you a place. They'll teach you how to use all kinds of weapons. You'll learn strategy and tactics—you know—the art of war. You'll become a real soldier. In no time you could be an officer."

The smile mechanically plastered across Picazo's face began to twitch at the edges.

José's eyes glanced around at the filth lining the church, *his* church. From nearby in the sanctuary, a rooster crowed. Hooves sounded lightly on the tile floor. Ever so carefully, he lifted his head until he stood level with Rafael Picazo's shoulders. Then he exhaled slowly. His lips were drawn taut in one fine line.

"I'd rather die. I joined the Cristeros to open up the churches again. I'll never fight for the persecutors of the Church."

Picazo gulped. His smile caved in. In its place, his face assumed a mask of steel.

"You know what this means, boy?"

~

The setting sun cast its last radiant colors across the sky. Shadows began to fill the baptistery.

Lorenzo sat in the corner, poking at his foot.

"Qué pasa?" asked José, tossing pebbles against the wall.

"It's just—I'm scared. What are they going to do with us?"

"I wish I knew. You heard my godfather this afternoon. He wants me to join his side and follow one of his crazy schemes."

"And why don't you?" Lorenzo broke in. "I mean, at least to get out of this prison. Once you're free, you can join the Cristeros again."

José shook his head. "No, Lorenzo. No, I can't. That would be denying everything I've been fighting for. I'd feel so hollow."

Lorenzo looked intently at José for a moment. "But what about me, José? I don't want to die."

"The truth is," said José, "neither do I."

∼

Rubbing his eyes, José sat up from where he had been sleeping. He let out a big yawn. Outside, the sun had not yet peeked above the horizon.

He stood up and stepped into the church. Movements near the altar caught his attention. There, on top of the tabernacle, sat a large rooster, its bright-red head clearly visible in the dim light. Another rooster sat on the altar, which was covered in filth. A third animal lay huddled, sleeping in a ball at the altar's foot.

"There, where you belong, Lord, they tie up their fighting roosters? No," José whispered, shaking his head.

He slipped back into the baptistery, careful not to disturb his little friend sleeping in the corner. A minute's worth of rubbing the rope that bound his hands on one of the rusty metal bars in the window snapped the cord.

"José?" came a voice from the darkness.

"Sorry to have woken you, Lorenzo."

"What are you up to?" the little boy asked.

"Someone tied his roosters up by the altar. I'm going to fix that."

"Ay José, what are you going to do? They'll kill us!"

"What does that matter? Jesus belongs up there, not animals. And death is a small thing. Heaven is what really matters."

He slipped out of the baptistery again and approached the bird sitting atop the tabernacle. Seeing him coming, the animal strutted about, but kept to its perch. As José stepped up level with the tabernacle, he spied a rope tying the rooster's foot to a brick. Reaching for the brick, he fiddled with the knot until it came undone. *I'll just let it go*, he thought, *and clean the tabernacle.*

He made as if to release the rope—then stopped. *And what's to stop it from coming back and making a mess again?*

Taking care to move slowly, José grabbed the animal and lifted it off the tabernacle, bringing its body under his arm. Holding its body with his right hand, he wrapped his left hand around its head, pinning its beak closed. Then he gave one firm tug, causing its neck to break. The bird burst into a fit of flapping. Half a minute later, it hung limp. He tossed the body to the ground.

Turning around, he made quick work of the other two animals. Then he stripped off his shirt and used it to clear the muck and feathers from the altar and the tabernacle.

"That's better," he said, surveying the scene. "I wonder whose birds they were?"

~

"Tonto! Do you know how much those birds were worth?"

Rafael Picazo's enraged face hovered inches away from José's. Lorenzo cowered in the corner.

José gulped.

"Answer me!" bellowed Picazo, glaring down at him.

"Godfather—" José started to speak.

"Don't call me that!" he interrupted. "I'm not your godfather anymore."

José could see the veins bulging on Picazo's neck. He hesitated.

"I said, 'Answer me!'" growled the angry man.

Clenching his fists, José turned and looked over at the altar of the church.

"The house of God is a place for prayer," he said, shaking his head, "not animals."

Picazo slammed his fist down on the marble baptismal font. "I gave you a chance to escape, and this is how you repay me? Your life is worth nothing to me now!" he shrieked.

José could see the soldier at Picazo's side playing with the bolt on his rifle. His own knees started to tremble. Swallowing hard, he unclenched his fists. "Then go ahead; I'm ready," he said, almost whispering. "Shoot me if you like and send me to God, and then I can ask him to confound you."

Picazo slapped José's cheek with the back of his hand, and the blow sent him staggering. "How dare you!" he shouted.

Lorenzo uttered a sob.

Turning on his heel, Picazo motioned to the soldier and marched off.

12

PAPÁ AND TÍA MAGDALENA

IN GUADALAJARA, a small, lanky boy beat his fist
against a door. "Señor Sánchez. Señora Sánchez. It's
me, Rafa, please open up."

Don Macario Sánchez undid a series of locks and
peered through the opening.

"Sorry I didn't answer your first knock, Rafa, it's
just that—"

"I don't have long. I came to deliver some news. The
Cristeros are saying that José was captured yesterday."

Don Macario swayed and grabbed the doorframe. "Where is he? Is he injured?"

Rafa hunched his shoulders. "I'm not sure. They—they bring most prisoners to Sahuayo, but no one has seen José yet. There'll be more news soon, I'm sure. It's best if you just wait here."

"Wait?" asked Don Macario, peering forward. "No. No I can't. I'll go find him." He started to close the door.

"But—but what about your family?" asked Rafa.

"They'll be safer here in Guadalajara."

~

Footsteps sounded again in the church.

"Someone's coming," said Lorenzo nervously.

José peered through the baptistery doorway. "Someone in white . . . not a soldier . . . *Tía Magdalena?*"

José's aunt strode into the baptistery unaccompanied.

"How did you get here?" José asked, throwing his arms around her.

"Let's just say I'm a neutral party," she said, peering into José's face. "What happened to your cheek, boy? Is that a bruise I see?"

"Señor Picazo . . ."

"My dear boy," said the woman, "we have to get you out of this place—both of you."

She drew a bag from her purse. "I brought you some food. There's rice and beans, a little chicken, and *agua de Jamaica*."

"You're the best, Tía," said José, accepting the gifts.

"And you are brave," she replied. "José, your father is on his way from Guadalajara to speak with Señor Picazo."

The boy's face lit up.

"He wants to get you out of here—maybe he'll—"

"Visiting time's over," said a voice from the corridor.

Magdalena sighed. "You take care of yourself. If you have any messages, send them to Tía María. Goodbye." She hugged both boys and disappeared round a corner.

"My, my," said José, digging around in the bag of food. "Tía Magdalena always outdoes herself. She didn't say anything about the tamales she managed to sneak in here."

He poked around some more and then whistled. "Not to mention the churros. Come on, Lorenzo, let's eat."

The other boy didn't move.

José took a bite from one of the churros.

"Heavenly," he murmured.

Lorenzo crossed his arms. "Your Papá is coming to rescue you," he said, "but my parents don't even know where I am."

José paused with the churro just inches from his lips.

"I'm sure that if they did know, they'd come for you too," he said, using his snack as a pointer. "Who knows, maybe my papá can get us both out."

Lorenzo was motionless.

"Here, have some food," said José, holding out the cinnamon-and-sugar-covered churro.

"I can't eat. I feel terrible," replied his friend.

José lowered himself to the ground beside Lorenzo.

"*Amigo*, all the pain will be gone in the blink of an eye, but heaven is forever."

His friend sat still.

"Come on. At least say grace with me."

"OK," answered Lorenzo.

"*Bendícenos, Señor, y bendice estos alimentos que por tu bondad vamos a tomar, por Cristo, nuestro Señor. Amén.*"

"Tastes good," murmured José, who had finished a second churro and started on the tamales. "Dinner's always better when you start with dessert."

Lorenzo peeked into Aunt Magdalena's bag of goodies.

Only the sound of munching came from José's direction.

"You win," said Lorenzo, finally smiling and unfolding his arms. "Let's try some of that chicken."

Both boys grabbed a drumstick.

"I wonder how those roosters would have tasted," mused Lorenzo between mouthfuls.

"Who knows," replied José, smiling. "They felt kind of rubbery to me."

13

LAZARUS

L ET GO OF HIM!'' shouted José.

Morning had come, and with it four soldiers who had stormed into the baptistery and roughly retied the boy's hands behind their backs. They dragged the two boys out into the town square, where one of the soldiers slipped a noose around Lorenzo's neck. The boy began to cry.

"No!" shouted José.

"One more peep and you'll regret it," barked a soldier, jabbing a rifle barrel into José's back.

Another soldier stood Lorenzo on a little stool and tied the other end of the rope around the low-hanging branch of a cedar tree.

"This is what we do to rebels!" shouted the officer in the group, and he nodded to the man holding the rope.

Burning-hot tears stole down José's cheeks as the man pulled the rope. José looked away. When he looked again at the tree, the soldiers were lowering Lorenzo to the ground.

Two of the soldiers put Lorenzo's lifeless body into a nearby donkey cart. The driver gave the donkey a whip, and the cart rolled off in the direction of the cemetery.

José started. "Wait, what about me?" he asked nervously.

"I thought I told you to shut up," snapped a soldier.

José watched the cart roll through the plaza until it turned the far corner and disappeared. Then the soldiers marched him back inside the church.

∼

"Here you go, old man, this one's freshly hanged," said the soldier, dropping the motionless body at the entrance to the cemetery.

Luis Gómez looked at the soldier, then back at the boy. He had dug more graves in the past month than the previous fifteen years. But what were soldiers doing with the body of a boy?

"Where do you want the grave?" asked the soldier. "The boss told me to help you dig, if you need it."

The gravedigger laid a hand on the boy's neck. He could have used some help, but—what was that? He thought he could feel a slight pulse.

"Oh, *no te preocupes*," he said, scratching his head. "They need you in town. I'll take care of him."

The soldier smiled. "Thanks, gravedigger man. I owe you one."

He jumped into the cart and gave the donkey a lash. The animal trotted off.

For a moment, the gravedigger made as if to dig the grave. Once the soldier had disappeared from sight, he hurried back and bent over the body. Yes, there was a pulse, though weak.

"Stupid soldiers can't even do a hanging right," he murmured under his breath.

Unscrewing the lid of his canteen, he took the boy's head in one hand, and with the other poured some water over Lorenzo's face.

The head shook a little, and then the lips parted in a yawn. Moments later, the eyelids fluttered and opened. The gravedigger gave a chuckle.

"Here, son, take a drink of this," he said, holding out the canteen.

"*Dónde . . .* where am I?" asked the boy, rubbing his face.

"You should be in a hole in the ground," answered the gravedigger.

A puzzled expression crossed Lorenzo's face. "Where is José?" he asked.

"You mean the Sánchez boy?"

"Yeah, him. We were prisoners together in the church."

The gravedigger shrugged. "What is your name, boy?" he asked.

"Lorenzo."

"Hmmm. I reckon we should give you a new name."

"Why's that?"

"Because you, my friend, are one lucky boy. By all rights, you should be dead. It's like you've been raised to life. We'll call you Lazarus."

The man offered the boy some of his food. After Lorenzo had gobbled down half the gravedigger's lunch, he asked, "Now what do I do?"

"*Váyate,*" replied the old man. "Get as far away from Sahuayo as you can. If you head due south you'll make Jiquilpan or even Los Remedios tonight. I'll dig you a nice grave and bury a stick at the bottom. The federales will never know the difference."

∽

In front of the baptismal font, José paced back and forth. Without Lorenzo, the night seemed to go on forever. *Why all the wait?*

"José, over here," said a voice at the window.

"Who's there?"

"It's me, Padre Ignacio."

José stood on the tips of his toes, barely managing to peer through the bars of the window.

"Boy, am I glad it's you, Padre. What are you doing out in the open? If the federales see you—"

"Did you think I'd stay holed up in hiding when my favorite nephew was all alone in jail? Besides, I hope you've been taking good care of the church for me. They're keeping you a prisoner here, but no one else is allowed near it."

"Ummm . . . let's just say that maybe you're better off not knowing what it's like in here," replied José, frowning.

"I figured as much," said the priest. "Did you hear about Lorenzo?"

José nodded, his face dropping.

"Miguel, the gravedigger, he says Lorenzo wasn't dead."

José looked up, startled. "What do you mean he wasn't dead? I saw him with my own eyes."

"Miguel says they dropped him off at the cemetery, but he was still alive. Somehow the federales didn't do their job right, *gracias a Dios*."

José put his face in his hands.

"I want to cry, Padre," he said, looking up. "Lorenzo was so afraid, and yet he faced death . . . and now he's free."

"Yes, everyone says it's a miracle; they're calling him Lazarus—it's like he was raised from the dead. He's already on his way to rejoin the Cristeros."

"Even if I never get out of here," said José, "I'll be happy, knowing that Lorenzo—I mean Lazarus—made it out. What about you, Padre? What have you been up to?"

"Oh, mostly saying Mass in people's homes and trying to keep up their hopes," said the priest with a sigh.

José's eyes brightened. "If you can say Mass, do you think I could receive Communion?" he asked.

"I don't know. This window's too high for me to bring it to you." The priest thought for a minute. "Maybe we could smuggle it in with your food or something."

"Yeah," said José excitedly. "Tía Magdalena brings me food sometimes."

"All right, next time she comes—" The priest suddenly stopped talking. Then he whispered, "Someone's coming. God bless you, son."

14

THE RANSOM

S O NICE TO SEE YOU, Señor Sánchez," said Rafael Picazo from behind his massive, oak desk.

Don Macario was still panting after jogging straight
from the train station to Picazo's office. Brown dust
clung to his white beard.

"Look, Señor Mayor," he said, once he had caught
his breath a little. "This is a terrible mistake. José's no
soldier. He doesn't belong in that prison."

"Ah, my dear Macario," replied Picazo. "I was inclined to think the same myself until I actually talked to the boy. I had assumed that the Cristeros tricked him into fighting. And of that I am still certain. But I also assumed that he didn't belong in prison. Last night, he destroyed some valuable property of mine. I know now that the boy's insolence has gotten him exactly what he deserves."

"But, Rafael, you're his godfather, for heaven's sake. Can't you just give the boy a chance? He's only fourteen."

"I gave him one chance," replied Picazo, "and he rejected it. Why should I give him another?"

"Because he's my son," replied Don Macario emphatically, "and I can't—I just can't lose him." He paused a moment, shaking his head. "Isn't there anything we can do?"

Rafael Picazo leaned back in his black leather chair and stared Don Macario in the eyes.

"I won't even consider letting the boy go," he said, taking a deep breath, "until you pay the ransom."

"Ransom? How much?"

"Oh, I don't know, somethinsg like five thousand gold pesos," he said, letting the last words tumble off his lips like stones into a pond.

"*Mercy*," mumbled Don Macario. "You know I don't have that kind of money."

"Well, if you value the boy's life, then you'd better find someone who does."

Ransom or no ransom, Rafael Picazo had no intention of letting José go free and gave the order for his execution to one of his henchmen.

"But, Rafael," said the man, "just think about the money."

"*No me importa*. You do your job, and you'll receive your pay."

"Whatever you say, Señor Mayor."

"My soldiers will bring the boy to the old rendezvous this evening," said Picazo. "After the bell rings for curfew, he's all yours. I don't care how you do it. All I ask is that come sunrise, there's one more body in the graveyard."

Later that evening four soldiers marched into the church, tied José by the hands, and pushed him outside. As soon as his feet touched the dust of the town square, his eyes shot to the cedar tree where Lorenzo had been hanged. But no noose hung from its branches.

They walked him past the tree, down the south side of the square, and turned left at the corner. After a few more steps, they came to a halt at the door of El Meson, an old inn. The blinds of the building were drawn, and on the façade, wooden lathing showed through missing chinks of plaster.

The soldier in front shoved the door open. "In here with the boy," he said.

The light from his lantern cast wavelike shadows down the walls within. In the middle of the room sat a long wooden table. Covered in cobwebs, a ramshackle chandelier dangled from the ceiling. Small piles of clutter were spread about the floor, much the same as at the church.

"What are you going to do with me?" asked José.

"You sit down here," said the soldier, motioning to a place beside the wall, "and keep quiet."

José shuffled over, hands still tied together, and carefully slid down the wall until he sat cross-legged on the damp floor. Back and forth, back and forth the soldiers walked, never speaking a word. After what felt like a small eternity, there came a knock. One of the men hurried over and swung the door inward.

"On your feet, prisoner," snapped a soldier.

José looked up, just in time to see his godfather enter the room.

"Everything in order, men?" asked Picazo, tossing the stub of a cigar to the ground and grinding it under his heel.

"Sí, Señor Mayor," said the man who had been carrying the lantern.

"*Bueno.*"

He walked up to the table and stopped just opposite José. After fumbling around in his pocket, he extracted a document.

"Let me see," he said, as his eyes scanned the paper. Without raising them, he added, "Aha, just as I thought. Listen, young man, to your death sentence."

> The committee has issued a sentence as regards one José Sánchez del Río, member of the insurrectionary force in open war with our esteemed government. For having been found guilty of high treason, the aforementioned rebel is to be put to death, without delay, to serve as an example to any who may feel inclined to join in so odious and unpatriotic an undertaking.

He slowly folded the paper and slipped it back into his pocket.

"They'll come for the boy at half past eight," said Picazo to the soldiers. "I want you to accompany them —make sure there are no mistakes."

José stared intently at Picazo's face. It betrayed no emotion—not even a twitch. After a weighty silence, the mayor turned to leave.

Just before he reached the door, José blurted out, "Can I send for a last meal?"

Picazo stopped. For a moment, he stood silent, as if hovering between two worlds. Then the moment passed.

"You," he said, motioning to the soldier nearest the door, "bring the prisoner pen and paper."

"And you," he continued, addressing another soldier. "Tell La Aguada that I want it done quietly."

With that, he stepped through the doorway and out into the darkening night.

～

The gold coins spilled from the sack and across the table onto the floor. Each piece glittered profusely in the lamplight.

"Five thousand. You can count it out: I'm sure it's there. Had to sell my house—and everything else."

"Impressive, Macario," said Rafael Picazo. "I admit I didn't think you quite up to the task."

Don Macario faked a smile. His fingers shone white as they clung tightly to the sack from which he had poured the coins. Dark bags hung from his eyes, and his shoes were caked with dust. His beard had grown scraggly and gray.

"It's all yours," he said. "Now—now give me my boy."

Picazo got to his feet and grabbed a handful of coins. He shook them back and forth in his palm, listening to the merry ring.

"You must understand me, Don Macario, when I say that these things take time," he stated somberly. "I'll need to file for a stay of execution; then if that's granted—"

"*If?*" exclaimed Don Macario. "You never told us there had been a sentence. For heaven's sake, Rafael," here he dropped his voice, "this is my son. Just let him go."

"Ah, Don Macario," said Picazo. "If only you would have chosen the right side in the first place, maybe your son wouldn't be in such a precarious position."

"Rafael, listen to me," Don Macario pleaded, drawing closer to the mayor. "Maybe you're right. Maybe I did make a mistake." He paused, laying a hand on his chest. "I can't change that now. But I can guarantee you that if you give me back my son, he won't cause you any more trouble."

Rafael Picazo smiled. Setting the coins down, he opened the top drawer of his desk and slowly pulled out a cigar. After lighting, he rang a bell on his desk.

A soldier walked in and saluted.

"Please show Señor Sánchez downstairs."

"Rafael, you can't do this," Don Macario said.

"I think we are finished here," replied Picazo, setting his feet up on the desk and motioning to the soldier.

"Rafael! Rafael!" Don Macario shouted as the soldier forcibly pushed him from the room and slammed the door behind him.

~

In the living room of the Sánchez del Río house in Guadalajara, Doña Mariquita sat by her youngest daughter.

"Mamá, do you think Papá will bring José back?" asked the girl.

"Oh Celia," replied Doña Mariquita. "I certainly hope so. Papá will do anything it takes."

"But what if José doesn't want to come?"

"What do you mean?"

"You remember what José said when he told us he was leaving, right?"

"He said a lot of things."

"Yes, but I remember one thing especially. Before José went off to join the Cristeros, he said, 'Winning heaven has never been so easy.'"

Mariquita looked her daughter in the eyes. "Celia dear, how did you hear that?"

The girl cocked her head to the side. "Because we were all on the stairs, listening, when he told you and Papá."

"I should have known," whispered Doña Mariquita.

"It'll be OK, Mamá," said Celia. "Just a day or two, and I'll have a brother in heaven."

Doña Mariquita took Celia in her arms. "Celia, dear, how can you say such a thing? Papá will bring José back safe and sound."

"Oh Mamá, you don't understand, do you? God gave you three daughters and four sons."

"What does that have to do with it, *tesoro*?" asked Doña Mariquita, looking deep into Celia's eyes.

"He gave you three daughters and three sons for you to watch over on this earth," answered the little girl, wrapping her arms around her mother, "and one to watch over you from heaven."

15

THE LAST COMMUNION

TREMBLING, José set down the pen. His heart beat relentlessly against his chest as he folded the letter closed.

Señora María Sanchez de Olmedo

My very dear Aunt,

I've been sentenced to death. At 8:30, the moment I have waited so long for will arrive. Thank you so much for all the favors that you and Magdalena did for me. I don't feel like I can write my mother. Can you please write her and María for me? The Lieutenant says Magdalena can come once more, can you please tell her? I think she'll come.

Say good-bye to everyone for me, and just like always and last of all, I give you all my love—you know how much I love you and want to see you.

Christ lives, Christ reigns, Christ rules. Viva Cristo Rey y Santa María de Guadalupe.

José Sánchez del Río, who died in defense of his faith

Don't forget to come.

Farewell.

Seeing that he had finished, the soldier on duty grabbed the letter with a grunt. After glancing at the name, he slipped from the room.

The other three soldiers stayed in their places.

Only ten minutes later, José heard voices outside.

"Can I see the boy? He's my nephew."

"Sorry, Señora, we've got orders," said a soldier. "I'll take that bundle for you."

"Men!" fumed the woman. She pushed the soldier aside and stuck her head through the doorway.

"I'm sorry, Señora, you're not allowed to—"

"Not allowed to what?" she snapped. "And you, Pedro Torres," she said to one of the men inside, "is this what I get for all the times I bandaged your scraped knees and carried you back to your mother? I would have thought better of you."

"Pedro, don't let her in," said the soldier at the door.

"But—" the other replied, shrugging his shoulders.

The man at the door threw his hands up in the air.

"You can come in, Señora Magdalena," said Pedro, "but make it short."

"That's better," she said and stepped inside. Her blue dress glowed in the feeble light.

José, who had been watching the scene unfold in silence, rose to his feet.

"You got my message?" he asked.

As she began to reply, she swung around to see three pairs of eyes and ears fixed in their direction.

"What about a little privacy?" she asked.

"Señora, we have to report to the mayor."

"What kind of cruel men are you? This is my nephew! Step outside for a moment so he and I can have a little heart-to-heart talk."

Grumbling to each other, the soldiers made their way out the door.

"Finally," she said, turning to José. "My dear boy..." She gave a deep sigh and hugged him tightly.

"Thank you for coming, Tía Magdalena."

"Oh José," she said, looking him in the eyes. She dropped her voice to a whisper, "I talked to the man who owns this building. He says there's a way out the back." She pointed to the door on their left.

José nodded. "Did you bring—"

The look of concern passed from the woman's face. She smiled, nodded, and took a small golden container from the bundle she was carrying.

"The Body of Christ," she said, holding up the little white Host.

A look of deep joy spread across José's face and lit up his features. "Amen."

～

José watched his aunt step through the door and into the night. From outside came voices—probably she was giving another lecture to the soldiers.

Her last words echoed in his head. Turning to his left, he faced the doorway she had spoken of. Now was his chance. He could escape and return to fight with the Cristeros.

He slipped over to the door. With a little pressure, the handle turned smoothly. Glancing over his shoulder, he took one last look. His aunt's voice still drifted through the air, but no one had entered the room yet.

His heart was pounding furiously against his ribcage. "Come on, come on," he whispered as he pushed on the door, hoping the hinges wouldn't squeak.

The door swung inward, and a second later he had stepped into a dark chamber. At the far end, he could see two more doors outlined against the wall. "The one on the right," Tía Magdalena had said.

José stepped forward. Simultaneously the door behind him swung shut and pitched the room into total darkness.

He kept his eyes turned toward where he had seen the door before and kept walking. Sure enough, after maybe ten steps, he could feel its outline.

Just a light push, and he had stepped into a small courtyard. Throbbing like a freight train, his heart felt as if it were lodged in his throat.

Far above, a waning moon shone brightly in the dark sky, casting down an eerie light, enough for José to see a few small trees and potted plants scattered about the courtyard.

As he took another step forward, a memory came to mind: a gunshot followed by a black figure falling to the ground.

"No," José gasped.

Suddenly his legs buckled. He turned and made his way back to his prison.

16

THE ROAD TO CALVARY

J OSÉ WAS BACK in his place against the wall when the
soldiers returned.

"What do you have to say for yourself?" asked one
of the men.

"Yeah, come on, you're just a kid," said another.

"You don't have to die," said a third. "All you have
to say is 'Long live President Calles', and we'll let you
go."

José only shook his head.

"Forget it," said the first man. "La Aguada will fix him."

Soon after the curfew bell rang, a gang of men arrived at the door. Out of their belts peeked revolvers. On their faces played twisted sneers. The soldiers let them in, and they drew up in a semicircle around José.

"So, kid," said a man with a rough beard, dangling a knife in José's face, "you better choose carefully, 'cause my blade don't like the looks of you."

So this must be La Aguada, thought José.

"Yeah," said another man, whose breath stunk of tequila. "Say, 'Long live President Calles', and we'll let you go free."

I don't even have to escape, José thought. *Just four words and I'm free.* Then his own advice to Lorenzo came echoing back in his ears: *The pain will be gone in the blink of an eye, but heaven is forever.*

"Viva Cristo Rey," said José.

No sooner had he closed his lips than the biggest of the thugs backhanded him across the face. "You sure about that?" he demanded.

José slowly wiped blood from the corner of his mouth and stared at his hand in silence. Then he nodded. Rough hands grabbed at him from every direction. The men lifted José from the ground and tossed him onto the table.

"You're not making things easy, boy," said Aguada, pointing his blade at José. "I can assure you that my knife isn't dull."

José frowned.

"So what do you say?"

José swallowed hard. "The same thing I said before," he answered, thinking of his friend hanging from the tree. "Viva Cristo Rey."

The man skinned José's feet. Then the men picked up the boy and set him down on the ground. José wriggled and winced in pain.

"What's that, have you had enough?" asked Aguada.

The boy nodded, but when he was told again to say what the men wanted to hear, he again refused.

The men shoved José out the door of the inn, and the boy lost his balance. With his hands still tied behind his back, there was nothing to stop his fall but the dirt. Luckily as he landed he rolled onto his side.

"*Qué pasa*—Cristero boy can't even keep his balance?" snickered one of the men.

José twisted his torso and managed to sit up. But no sooner had he started pushing with his feet to stand up than the pain made him stop. The men only laughed.

"Quiet, boys—Picazo wants us to keep this secret," said Aguada, and the laughter died down.

By now José was using his head to lift himself up. He pressed it into the dirt and managed to rise to his knees. He lifted his right leg and ever so slowly set his foot upon the ground. The pain made him lurch sideways and almost fall again.

"March," said Aguada.

José took one step forward. The terrible burning

sensation shooting up from his feet made him stumble again. He hopped from foot to foot, but instead of lessening, the pain only grew worse. He wanted to cry out.

"What kind of soldier are you?" asked another of the thugs, Pispírria, mockingly. "I knew the Cristeros were just a bunch of weaklings."

"Viva Cristo Rey," said José.

"Look, boy," said Aguada, "I told you not to say that."

"I say we make him pay for every word he says," declared Malpolá, switchblade in hand. He made as if to slash at José, but Aguada grabbed his hand.

"*Basta*," he said. "Wait till the cemetery."

～

Rafael Picazo stood at the window of his third-floor office overlooking the town square. He glanced at his watch: 11:15. They were behind schedule.

"What is wrong with those fools?" he wondered aloud.

He scanned the square again. The lampposts cast pools of yellow light on the pavement below. He was proud of those lampposts—they were his first project as mayor, back before the war. He had plans for beautifying and modernizing Sahuayo even more once the war was over.

Something moved in the far corner of the square. It was Picazo's men finally arriving with José. The ruffians walked before and behind the boy, and the soldiers marched on either side of him with rifles at their hips. Through the closed window Picazo could hear shouting.

"The *idiotas* better keep quiet," he muttered, "or the whole town will be out to see."

The clamor grew louder as the procession wound its way across the south side of the square and then headed north. When Picazo opened his window he realized it wasn't the soldiers who were making the noise.

"Viva Cristo Rey!"

The blood drained from his face. He slammed his fist on the wall. Rushing out of his office, he headed for the stairs. As he pulled open the front door of the building, he saw the group turning the corner.

"*Párate!*" he shouted, hurrying down the front steps.

The soldiers stopped, as did the men in front and back.

"I thought I told you to keep it quiet," Picazo said.

"We're not making the noise—he is," said one of the men, pointing to José.

Picazo pushed his way past the soldiers.

José turned to face him.

"Look, boy, I've already been too nice with you. I'm giving you one last chance. Say 'Death to Christ the King' or you'll wish you had later."

José opened his mouth as if to speak, but no words

came. The boy's eyes were fixed on a spot beyond Picazo's left shoulder, where two figures were moving in the shadows: Padre Ignacio and Trino.

"Answer me, boy—now!"

"Viva Cristo Rey y Santa María de Guadalupe!"

"Give me that rifle," barked Picazo to one of the soldiers.

Crack!

Padre Ignacio and Trino winced as Picazo crashed the rifle into José's jaw.

"That'll keep you quiet," he said.

Trino was livid. "That's it, I'm going in there," he said, getting to his feet.

Padre Ignacio grabbed him by the arm. "No, you're not," he said. "They'll kill you too."

Trino dropped back down on one knee.

"Look," said Padre Ignacio, pointing. "There goes Picazo back to his den. They've started moving again."

"Let's follow them," Trino suggested.

The priest nodded, and they started off. They hung close to the wall, watching as the group of soldiers left the square and headed down Constitution Street. By the time Trino and the padre reached the place where Picazo had hit José, the group was already a block away.

"Look," said Trino, stooping down and placing a hand on the ground. "José's footprints—they're red."

Padre Ignacio gasped. "Murderers!"

17

WINNING HEAVEN

W HERE'S THAT GRAVEDIGGER?" demanded Aguada. "Over here, sir," said a voice from the middle of the graveyard.

The men marched off, pushing José from behind.

As they came to where the old man stood, Aguada threw up his hands in impatience.

"Where's the grave?"

"Orders of Señor Picazo, sir," replied the man. "The

prisoner is to dig his own grave. I'm only allowed to fill it in."

Aguada laughed. "The mayor sure has imagination."

"Here's a shovel," said the gravedigger, holding out a small spade.

"You heard the man, boy. Get to work," Aguada demanded.

José hobbled forward, hands tied behind his back.

"You might want to free the prisoner's hands," observed the gravedigger.

"Mind your own business," snapped Aguada. He turned and made a nod with his head.

A man with a knife lumbered over and grabbed José by the wrists. A quick slice, and the rope fell to the ground. José slowly brought his arms forward until they hung like weights at his side.

"OK, boy," shouted Malpolá, giving José a kick from behind, "start digging!"

José reeled forward. The gravedigger reached out to stop him from falling and grabbed him with both arms. Then he set the boy back on his feet. Trembling himself, he took first one, then the other, of José's hands and wrapped them around the handle of the shovel. He pointed to an "x" marked on the ground.

José feebly scraped at the dirt.

"Looks like he could use some encouragement," said Malpolá, knife at the ready.

Aguada held up a hand.

At first José only scratched ineffectively at the soil.

Then ever so slowly, he managed to grip the shovel tighter. Blood began to flow back into his fingers. Each scoop removed a little pile of dirt.

The cloud was clearing from his mind now. *I'm digging my grave. My own grave*, he thought. *Heaven. Almost there. Almost.* He paused, suddenly feeling nauseated, and placed a hand on his stomach.

"Snap out of it, boy," shouted Aguada.

He gripped the shovel again and resumed the digging. *José*, said a little voice in his head, *you don't have to do this. You've already suffered enough. Just give in; walk away. You can still be a Cristero.*

José peered around. The men were all still there, laughing and joking. Where did the voice come from?

Just drop the shovel and walk away, said the voice. *It's so easy.*

José shook his head, trying to think clearly. Just then, he heard the soldiers mention a name, a name he remembered. Still digging, he listened.

"Where is his grave, old man?" asked one of the soldiers.

"It's this one, right here," said the gravedigger, pointing to a mound of dirt. "Dug the grave with my own hands."

A smile slowly stole its way across José's face as he thought of Lorenzo, not buried there as the soldiers thought, but safe from them, miles away.

Then he swallowed and opened his lips. "I need to pray," he whispered. "Viva Cristo Rey."

"What's that, boy?" asked Malpolá.

"Viva Cristo Rey," answered José.

"Stop it," snapped Aguada.

"Viva Cristo Rey," José stated emphatically.

The men drew closer round the boy, who continued his digging.

"Viva Cristo Rey," he said, louder this time.

"*Basta*," said Malpolá.

He nodded to Pispírria. They both pulled out their knives, as did Zamorano and Chiscuasa.

Shovel still in hand, José gazed at the men with their weapons. "No matter what you do to me," he said, stealing a quick glance at Lorenzo's grave, "every time I move it means 'Viva Cristo Rey.'"

The men stepped forward, closing the knot tight around the boy. Without waiting, they let their blows rain down upon his body. He fell to the ground.

"Give up yet?" demanded Aguada.

The attack knocked José down on his back. He scrambled to his knees and stared at the blood dripping down his arms and over his hands. In the same instant, José saw the big crucifix in church, the one with the blood dripping from Jesus' wounds. Leaning over, he dragged his own bloody finger in the dust: first sideways, then up and down. A bloody cross. Then, carefully, painfully, he repeated his cry, "Viva Cristo Rey y Santa María de Guadalupe."

Aguada walked up behind the kneeling boy, his palm clutching a small wooden-handled pistol.

"*Niño*, what do you want me to tell your father?" he asked, slowly raising his weapon.

Joining his hands together, as if in prayer, José raised his head and said, "That we'll see each other in heaven." Then, taking a deep breath, he added with a shout, "Viva Cristo Rey y Santa María de Guadalupe!"

As the echoes of José's last cry carried through the air, a shot rang out. He lay still.

It was half an hour to midnight, February 10, 1928.

As the ruffians walked back, laughing, to report to Picazo, they were surprised to see people in the streets. There were people everywhere: people weeping, people kneeling, people gathering small handfuls of the damp red earth. From every direction, their whispers echoed one word: "Martyr."

18

THE WAY OF SAINTHOOD

T HREE YEARS LATER, Rafael Picazo was on the train
from Mexico City to Sahuayo.

"I'd trade México City for Sahuayo any day," said
his travelling companion.

"So would I," said Picazo, "but still, nothing beats
being mayor. It's like I'm king."

"Ha, ha, and what a kingdom you have. Dusty
streets, buildings falling apart, peasants and their
fears . . ."

"Oh, please," snapped Picazo. "When you get as much power as me, you might start enjoying life. Until then, just let me do my job."

The train rumbled on. The two men sat in silence, staring out the window. Unnoticed to both, a third figure slipped into the compartment.

"Rafael Picazo?" asked the man.

Both men turned and stared at the newcomer. A look of surprise stole across Picazo's face.

"Manuel Gallardo—funny running into you here," he said uneasily.

"Then you must be the only one laughing, as usual," said the man, drawing a revolver from his belt.

Picazo scooted back against the wall of the compartment, cautiously raising his hands in the air.

"Whoa, wait a minute. Manuel, we can talk about this," he protested.

"Talk?" asked the man. "I think we've talked enough. You can't seem to keep your nose out of my business, and I'm going to make sure you don't have another chance."

Bang! The man fired the gun and ran from the compartment. Enrique knelt at the side of his mortally wounded friend as other passengers began to gather around him.

"Rafael, Rafael, stay with me," shouted Enrique.

"I . . . I . . . I want—" mumbled Picazo.

"Yes, yes, what is it?" asked Enrique, holding his friend's hand.

"Enrique, get me a priest. I want a priest," gasped the dying man.

"For God's sake, Rafael, how am I supposed to find a priest here?"

"I am a priest," said a voice from behind them. Enrique turned and saw a man dressed like a peasant stepping from the crowd.

"I'm Padre Ramón Martínez."

"Padre," whispered Rafael Picazo softly, "would you please hear my confession?"

~

There he was again, crying in the back of church. He would walk from statue to statue, image to image, the tears streaming from his eyes.

"Who's that man?" a little boy asked his mother from their pew.

"He's called La Aguada, son," the woman replied, holding her child close. "He's very sorry for some bad things he once did."

"Like that old man who walks around town all sad?" asked the boy.

"Yes, that's El Zamorano," she said. "He has asked God for forgiveness too. They say he has a great devotion to the Sacred Heart and goes to daily Mass now."

"It's sad that they did the bad things," said the little boy, "but I'm happy they have come back to Jesus."

"Yes," said the woman, "it's a miracle of sorts—they and all their friends have repented of what they did years ago."

~

Seventy-seven years later, the sky shone blood-red in the rays of the setting sun. Not a seat was left in the soccer stadium that day, November 20, 2005. But no soccer players could be seen driving any balls down the grassy field. The crowd of seventy thousand was cheering, but not for any athlete.

It was the beatification ceremony of thirteen martyrs, among them a fourteen-year-old boy from Sahuayo. He was being declared Blessed—the last step before becoming a saint—along with the man at whose tomb he had prayed for the grace of martyrdom.

The cardinal's words echoed throughout the stadium:

> For his heroism and his young age, José Sánchez del Río deserves special mention. He was from Sahuayo in Michoacán, and at the age of fourteen he bore valiant witness to Jesus Christ. He was an exemplary son, who shone for his obedience, reverence, and spirit of service. He wanted to be a martyr for Christ from the very beginning of the persecution.
>
> He shocked those who knew him, for he was so eager to give his blood for Christ. He received the martyr's crown after being tortured and after sending

his parents one last message: "We'll see each other in heaven. Viva Cristo Rey y Santa María de Guadalupe!"

The young Blessed José Sánchez del Río should inspire us all, especially you young people, who are able to give witness to Christ in your day-to-day life. Dear young people, Christ probably won't ask you to spill your blood, but he certainly does ask you, from today on, to give witness with the truth of your lives (Jn 18:37) in the midst of an environment of indifference to transcendental values and of materialism and hedonism that attempt to suffocate our consciences. Christ hopes, moreover, for your openness in accepting a vocation prepared for you by him. Only he has the answers to the questions that each of us asks, and he invites you to follow him in married, priestly, or religious life.[1]

~

It was standing room only in Saint Peter's Square. People from all over the world had gathered to celebrate the canonization of seven new saints. Tapestries with their images hung from the façade of Saint Peter's Basilica. Two tapestries were for bishops, three for priests, one for a nun, and one tapestry showed the image of a boy dressed in blue jeans. In his hand he carried a palm branch—the symbol of martyrdom.

[1] Cardinal José Saraiva Martins, homily, Mass of Beatification of Thirteen Mexican Martyrs (November 20, 2005), no. 6, http://www.vatican.va/roman _curia/congregations/csaints/documents/rc_con_csaints_doc_20051120_beati ficazioni_sp.html, translated by the author.

Pope Francis stood beneath the larger-than-life tapestries of the new saints and read the official declaration that named the fourteen-year-old martyr from Sahuayo Saint José.

How did this happen?

Once his martyrdom was verified, José was quickly beatified. But to be declared a saint, a miracle was needed. Literally. To be made a saint is such a huge honor that the pope will give someone that title only after proof of heavenly intervention. Three years after José's beatification, heaven did intervene and saved the life of a baby girl.

Her name was Ximena. Shortly after birth, she ran a fever that baffled the doctors. After days of testing, they discovered that she was suffering from atypical pneumonia and that one of her lungs was filled with fluid. A hurried operation followed, saving Ximena from pneumonia, but the doctors found that she was also suffering from tuberculosis. Then little Ximena suffered a stroke that, according to scans, damaged 90 percent of her brain.

Ximena spent the next seventy-two hours in a doctor-induced coma, attached to a respirator and other machines. During that time, her parents went to Mass daily and prayed to God for a cure. They also asked for the prayers of their favorite patron, José Sánchez del Río—"Joselíto" as they called him affectionately. Ximena's mother was born in Sahuayo, and she had long felt a special devotion to her hometown's young martyr.

As they disconnected Ximena from the life-support machines, the doctors warned her mother that the little girl would never recover the full use of her mind and body and would most likely die. To the surprise of all, the first thing the baby did was to open her eyes and smile.

A complete cure came quickly. First the doctors registered 80 percent brain activity, followed by an astonishing 100 percent. Warned that her daughter would not be able to eat or drink, the delighted mother watched as her baby girl drank eight ounces from a bottle. Ximena was completely cured.

One of the doctors told her mother, "The case of your daughter is a miracle." After long examination and further testing, the Vatican accepted Ximena's cure as a miracle worked through the intercession of José Sánchez del Río. Ximena brought up the gifts during José's canonization Mass on October 16, 2016.

The fourteen-year-old boy whose faith meant more to him than life is now a model of virtue for all people and all nations. Saint José, martyr for the faith, heavenly intercessor, pray for us!

AUTHOR'S NOTE

I'll never forget that day. It was sixth grade. Brother Eric, a seminarian, was substitute-teaching religion class. But instead of the usual catechism lesson, he told us the story of a Mexican boy who was martyred for his faith and never stopped shouting, "Long live Christ the King!" When I heard about this fourteen-year-old boy, explosions went off in my twelve-year-old heart. If José could give his life for God, then I could do something for God too. Inspired by him, I joined the seminary, one of the best decisions I ever made. Thank you, José!

When I looked for more about José, I couldn't find a single book about him in English. That was 1993. In 2004, I decided it was time for me to put his story in writing. This book is the result of ten years of research, during which time I obtained copies of what I believe to be every historical document ever written about José.

The main source for information on his life is the document prepared for his beatification process and given to the Congregation for the Causes of Saints in Rome. It is called a *Positio* and contains a biographical sketch, witnesses' testimony, and anything written by José. My other main sources were the two most extensive books written about José: *Los Gallos de Picazo o los Derechos de Dios*, by Father Luis Laureán Cervantes, and *Vida, Muerte, y Beatificatión del Niño Mártir José Sánchez del Río*, by Father Javier Villaseñor Castellanos.

We also have a few telegrams written by federal and Cristero generals about the three battles and skirmishes in which José took part. The first was the battle of Los Cutos as described in chapter 9 above. The second was the raid by federal troops during Mass as described above in chapter 10. The third was his capture during an ambush by federal troops on February 5, 1928.

I could have used the results of my ten years of research to write a history book. But I wanted the life of Saint José to come alive for young people as it came alive for me when I first heard his story. So I took all the research I had done and put it together in dramatized form.

We have only two letters and very few actual quotes from José. Many parts of his life are simply not mentioned by the witnesses. To write a cohesive story, I used everything we have, and then filled in the blanks. Sometimes I relied on local legend, at other times I made connections of my own, and often I just had to put myself in the mindset of a fourteen-year-old boy again.

I would like to thank Emilio Martínez for his research and my mom, Theresa McKenzie, for hers.

Many thanks as well to my dad, Bill McKenzie, for his many proofreads. Thanks, too, to all those who have helped edit and proofread, especially Lisa Cusmano, Father Daniel Brandenburg, and the editors at Ignatius Press. You all helped make it a much better book! Thanks as well to Father Joel Castañeda, Father Juan Pablo Ledesma, Father Luis Manuel Laureán, Father Nicholas Sheehy, Father Randall Meissen, Father Paul Alger, Father James Perez, and my sister Marianne for their help and advice.

Discovering the story of José's life has been a rewarding adventure. I hope he comes to life in these pages for you, the reader, as he has for me. He is a powerful intercessor and heavenly friend, and an inspiration for us all. Viva Cristo Rey!